# SELECTED

# CORRESPONDENCE

OF

## GUSTAVE FLAUBERT

WITH AN

INTIMATE STUDY OF THE AUTHOR

BY

## CAROLINE COMMANVILLE

**WILDSIDE PRESS**

Published by
Wildside Press, LLC
P.O. Box 301
Holicong, PA 18928-0301 USA
www.wildsidepress.com


Wildside Press Edition: MMIII

# INTIMATE REMEMBRANCES

OF

## GUSTAVE FLAUBERT

### I.

HESE pages are not a biography of Gustave Flaubert, they are simply recollections; my own and those I have collected.

My uncle's life was passed entirely in the intimacy of the family, between his mother and me; to relate the story of this life is to make him better known, more loved and esteemed; in this way I believe that I am fulfilling a pious duty towards his memory.

Before Gustave Flaubert's birth, my grandparents had had three children. The eldest, Achilles, was nine years older than Gustave, and the two other little ones were dead. Then came Gustave and another boy who died in a few months; and finally my mother, Caroline, the last child.

She and her younger brother loved each other with a peculiar tenderness. With but three years difference in their ages, the two little ones were scarcely ever separated from each other. Gustave repeated everything he learned to his sister; she was his pupil, and one of his greatest pleasures was initiating her into literary composition. Later, when he was in Paris, it was to her he wrote; through her was the daily news transmitted to their parents, because that sweet communion had not been lost.

I should say that the greater part of the facts relative to my uncle's infancy have been told me by the old nurse who brought him up and who died three years after him, in 1883. The familiarity permitted with a child was followed in her case by a respect and worship for her master. She was "full of him," recalling his least action, his least word. When she said "Monsieur Gustave," she believed that she was speaking of an extraordinary being. Those who knew him will appreciate the verity contained in the admiration of this old servant.

Gustave Flaubert was four years old when Julie came to Rouen into my grand-parents' service, in 1825. She came from the village of Fleury-on-the-Andelle, situated in that pretty, smiling valley which extends from Pont-Saint-Pierre to the great market-town of Lyons-la-Forêt. The coast of the "Two Lovers" protected its entrance; here and there was a château, sometimes surrounded by water and having its drawbridge, again the superb estate of Radepont, the ruins of an old abbey and the woods of the surrounding hills.

This charming country is fertile in old stories of love and of ghosts. Julie knew them all. She was a skilful story-teller, this simple girl of the people, and endowed with a naturally fine and agreeable mind. Her ancestors, from father to son, had been postilions, rather bad fellows, and hard drinkers,

While Gustave was small he would sit beside her for whole days. In order to amuse him, Julie would join together all the legends she had heard around the fire with those she had read, and, having been kept in bed a year with a bad knee, she had read more than most women of her class.

The child was of a tranquil nature, meditative, possessing an ingenuousness of which he retained traces during his whole life. My grandmother has told me that he would remain for hours with a finger in his mouth, absorbed, and with an almost stupid appearance. When he was six years old an old domestic, called Pierre, used to amuse himself with that innocence; he would say to little Gustave, if he teased for anything, "Go now and look at the end of the garden, or in the kitchen and see whether I am there." And the child would go and say to the cook: "Pierre sent me to see whether he were here." He could not comprehend that they were deceiving him, and while they laughed, would stand thinking, trying to see through the mystery.

My grandmother had taught her oldest son to read, and, wishing to do as much for the second, put herself to the task. The little Caroline, beside Gustave, learned by degrees that she could not keep up with him, and he, being forced to understand this from signs of which no one said anything to him, began to weep large tears. He was, however, eager for knowledge, and his brain worked continually.

Opposite the hospital, in a modest little house in the Rue de Lecat, lived two old people, Father and Mother Mignot. They had an extreme tenderness for their little neighbour. Times without number, the child would open the heavy door of the Hôtel-Dieu, and run across to Father Mignot's knee, upon a signal from him. And it was not the good woman's strawberries that tempted him, but the stories the old man told him. He knew a great many pretty tales of one kind and another, and with what patience he related them! From this time Julie was supplanted. The child was not difficult to please, but had insistent preferences; those that he liked must be told him over and over again.

Father Mignot also read to him. *Don Quixote* especially pleased my uncle; he would never let it be taken from him. And he retained for Cervantes the same admiration all his life.

In the scenes brought about by the difficulty of learning to read, the last irrefutable argument with him was: "Why should I learn, since Papa Mignot can read to me?"

But the age for entering school arrived. He must know once for all that his old friend could not follow him there. Gustave put himself resolutely to work, and at the end of a few months had caught up with the children of his age. He entered the eighth class.

He was not what one would call a brilliant pupil. Continually failing to observe some rule, and not troubling himself to understand his professors, punishments abounded, and the first prize escaped him, except in history, in which he was always first. In philosophy he distinguished himself, but he never comprehended mathematics.

Generous and full of exuberance, he had some warm friends whom he amused extremely by his unquenchable enthusiasm and good humour. His melancholy times, for he had them even then, he passed in a region of his mind accessible to himself alone, and not yet did he show them in his exterior life. He had a great memory, forgetting nothing, neither benevolences nor vexation of which he was the subject. Thus, he preserved for his professor in history, Cheruel, a profound remembrance, and hated a certain usher who had hindered him from reading his favourite book during the study hour.

But his years at the college were miserable; he never could become accustomed to things there, having a horror of discipline, and of everything that savoured of militarism. The custom of announcing the change of exercises by the beating of drums irritated him, and that of filing the pupils in rank when they passed from one class to another exasperated him. Constraint in his movements was a punishment, and his walk with the procession every Thursday was never a pleasure; not that he was feeble, but he had a natural antipathy for all that seemed to him useless motion. His antipathy for walking lasted his whole life. Of all exercises for the body, swimming alone pleased him; he was a very good swimmer.

The dull, labourious days of school life were enlivened by outings on Thursdays and Sundays. Then he saw his beloved family and his little sister, which was a joy unequalled.

In the dormitory during the week, thanks to some hidden pieces of candle, he read some of Victor Hugo's dramas, and his passion for the theatre was kept warm. From the age of ten, Gustave composed tragedies. These pieces, of which he was scarcely able to write the lines, were played by him and his comrades. A great billiard hall opening from the salon was given up to them. The billiard table, pushed to one end of the room, served as a stage, which they mounted by means of a crock from the garden. Caroline had charge of the decorations and costumes. His mother's wardrobe was plundered for old shawls, which made excellent peplums. He wrote to one of his principal actors, Ernest Chevalier: "Victory! victory! victory! victory! You will come, and Amédée, Edmond, Madame Chevalier, Mamma, two servants and perhaps some pupils, will be here to see us play. We shall give four pieces that you do not know. But you will soon learn them. The tickets of the first, second, and third classes are made. There will be some armchairs. There will also be scenery and decorations; the curtain is arranged. Perhaps there will be ten or twelve persons. So we must have courage and not fear," etc.

Alfred Le Poittevin, some years older than Gustave, and his sister Laura, were also a part of these representations. The family of Poittevin was bound to that of Flaubert through the two mothers, who had known each other from nine years of age at the *pension*. Alfred Le Poittevin had a very great influence upon my uncle in his youth, contributing to his literary development. He was endowed with a brilliant mind, full of life and eccentricity. He died young, which was a great grief. My uncle speaks of him in his preface to the *Last Songs*.

A few words about my grandparents and upon the moral and intellectual development of my uncle.

My grandfather, whose traits have been sketched in *Madame Bovary*, under those of Doctor Larivière, called in consultation to the bed of the dying Emma, was the son of a veterinary of Nogent-on-the-Seine.

The situation of the family was modest: nevertheless, by denying themselves, they sent their son to Paris to study medicine. He took the first prize in the great competition and by this success was received as a doctor free of further cost. Scarcely had he passed his examinations when he was sent from Dupuytren, where he was house physician, to Rouen to Doctor Laumonier, who was then surgeon of the hospital. This sojourn was supposed to be only temporary, to restore his health, which had become enfeebled from overwork and a life of privation. But, instead of re-maining for a few months, the young physician spent all his life there. The frequent appeals of his numer-ous friends, or the hope of arriving at a high place in the medical profession in Paris, which his success-ful beginning had justified, never decided him to leave his hospital and a people to whom he became profoundly attached.

But in the beginning, it was love which extended this sojourn,—love for a young girl, a child of thir-teen years, a goddaughter of Madame Laumonier, an orphan in a boarding-school, who came each week to visit her godmother.

Anne-Justine-Caroline Fleuriot was born in 1794 at Pont-l'Evêque in Calvados. Through her mother she was allied to the oldest families in Lower Nor-mandy. "A great noise is made," said Charlotte Corday in one of her letters, "about an unequal mar-riage between Charlotte Cambremer de Croixmare and Jean-Baptiste Francois-Prosper Fleuriot, a doctor without reputation." At thirty years of age Mademoi-selle de Croixmare had been sent back to the con-vent. But the obstacles were finally conquered, the walls of the convent broken and the marriage took place. One year later a daughter was born, and the mother died in giving her birth.

The child, left in the arms of its father, became for him an object of tenderness and worship. At sixteen, my grandmother still remembered with emotion her father's kisses. "He would undress me each evening," she said, "and put me in my bed, wishing to take my mother's place." These paternal cares soon ceased. Doctor Fleuriot, seeing that he was about to die, gave his daughter in charge of two old ladies of Saint-Cyr who had a little school at Honfleur. These ladies promised to keep her until her marriage, but they, too, soon disappeared. Then her tutor, Monsieur Thouret, sent the young girl to Madame Laumonier, sister of Jacques-Guillaume Thouret, Deputy from Rouen to the States-General and President of that Assembly. She came at the same time as my grandfather, when they happened to see each other. Some months later they avowed their love and promised themselves to each another.

The Laumonier household, like many others of that epoch, tolerated, under a spiritual and gracious exterior, a certain lightness of morals. The eminently serious nature of my grandmother and her love preserved her from the dangers of such surroundings. Besides, my grandfather, more far-seeing than she could be, wished her to remain in the boarding-school until she was married. She was eighteen and he twenty-seven at the time of their marriage. Their purse was slender, but their hearts had little fear. My grandfather's portion was in his future; my grandmother had a little farm which brought her a revenue of four thousand francs.

The household was established in the Rue du

Petit-Salut, near the Rue Grand-Pont, a little street of narrow houses, touching one another, where the sun could never penetrate. In my childhood my grandmother would often take me through there, and, looking at the windows, would say in a grave voice, almost religious: "Look, my child, the best years of my life were passed there."

Descended from a Champenois and a Norman, Gustave Flaubert had the characteristic signs of both races; his temperament was very expansive and, at the same time, it was enveloped in the vague melancholy of the people of the north. He was of even temper and gay, sometimes with a touch of buffoonery; but ever at the bottom of his nature was an undefined sadness, a kind of disquiet. He was physically robust, enjoying full, strong pleasures; but his soul, aspiring to an unattainable ideal, suffered without ceasing in not finding it. This applied to the smallest things; because, as a seeker after the exquisite, he had found that the most frequently recurring sentiment was nearly always one of grief. This without doubt added to the sensibility of his nervous system, which the violent commotions of a certain malady (to the paroxysms of which he had had many relapses, especially in his youth) had refined to an extreme point. That came also from his great love of the ideal. This nervous malady threw a veil over his whole life; it was a permanent fear obscuring even his happiest days. However, it had no influence upon his robust health, and the incessant and vigorous work of his brain continued without interruption.

Gustave Flaubert was something of a fanatic; he had taken art for his god, and like a devotee, he knew all the tortures and all the intoxications of the love to which he had sacrificed himself. After hours passed in communion with abstract form, the mystic became man again, was a *bon vivant,* laughed with a frank laugh, put a charming gaiety into the recital of a story, or some pleasant personal remembrance. One of his greatest pleasures was to amuse those about him. What would he not do to raise my spirits when I was sad or ill?

It was easy to feel the honesty of his characteristics. From his father he had received his tendency to experiment, that minute observation of things which caused him to spend infinite time in accounting to himself for the smallest detail, and that taste for all knowledge which made him a scholar as well as an artist. His mother transmitted to him his impressionability and that almost feminine tenderness which often made his great heart overflow and his eyes grow moist at the sight of a child. His taste for travel, he often said, came to him from one of his ancestors who took part in the conquest of Canada. He was very proud of counting up the brave ones among his own people, any one who had brains and was not *bourgeois;* for he had a hatred of the *bourgeois,* and continually employed that term as a synonym for mediocrity and envy, the living only with the appearance of virtue and insulting all grandeur and beauty.

At the death of Laumonier, my grandfather succeeded him as surgeon-in-chief of the Hospital. It was in this vast building that Gustave Flaubert was born.

The Hospital at Rouen, of the construction of the last century, is not wanting in a certain kind of character; the straight lines of its architecture present something of chasteness and something of the accepted modern types. It was situated at the end of Rue de Crosne, and as one came from the centre of the town he found himself face to face with the great arch of the iron gate, all black, behind which was a court-yard with willows planted in rows: at the end and built around the sides was the edifice.

The part occupied by my grandparents formed a wing, approached by a private entrance. At the left of the central gate, a high door opened upon a court where grass grew among the old paving stones. On the other side of, the pavilion was a garden forming an angle with the street, bordered at the left by a wall covered with ivy and hemmed in at the right by the hospital buildings. These are high grey walls, punctured with little glazed holes to which meagre faces are glued, their heads bound in white linen cloths. These ghastly silhouettes with hollow eyes show great suffering and have a profound sadness about them.

. Gustave's room was on the side of the entrance, in the second story. The view was upon the hospital gardens overlooking the trees, under whose verdure the patients sat on stone seats, when the weather was pleasant. From time to time the white wing of a great bonnet of one of the sisters could be seen rapidly crossing the courtyard, and sometimes there were visitors, the parents of the invalids, or the friends of the attendants, but never any noise or anything unexpected.

This severe and melancholy place could not have been without influence upon Gustave Flaubert. He ever retained an exquisite compassion for all human suffering, and also a high morality, which would scarcely be suspected by those who are scandalised by his paradoxes.

No one was less like what is usually called an artist than my uncle. Among the peculiarities of his character, the contrasts have always astonished me. This man, so preoccupied with beauty in style and giving form so high a place, even the highest, paid little attention to the beauty that surrounded him; his own furniture was of heavy contour, not the least delicate, and he had no taste for objects of art (bric-à-brac) so much in vogue at that time.

He loved order with a passion, carrying it to a mania, and would never work until his books were arranged in a certain fashion. He preserved carefully all letters addressed to him. I have large boxes full of them. Did he think there would be as much interest taken in them as there was later in his own? Did he foresee that great interest in his correspondence (which reveals the man in a light so different from that revealed by his works), that he imposed upon me the task of collecting and publishing it? No one can say.

He always observed extreme regularity in his work each day. He yoked himself to it as an ox is yoked to a cart, without waiting for that inspiration which expectation renders fruitless, as he said. His energy of will for all that concerned his art was prodigious, and his patience was tireless. Some years before his death, he would amuse himself by saying: "I am the last of the Fathers of the Church," and, in fact, with his long, maroon-coloured wrapper and a little black silk cap on the top of his head, he was something like a recluse of Port-Royal,

I can see him now running over the terrace at Croisset, absorbed in thought, stopping suddenly, his arms crossed, raising his head and remaining for some moments with his eyes fixed on the space above, and then resuming his walk again.

Life at the Hospital was regular, free, and good. My grandfather, who had attained a high reputation, medically, gave his children all that ease and tenderness could add to the happiness of youth. He had bought a house in the country, at Deville near Rouen, which he disposed of one year before his death, a railroad having cut through the garden only a few metres from the house. It was then that he bought Croisset, on the banks of the Seine.

Each year the entire family went to Nogent-on-the Seine to the home of the Flaubert parents. It was quite a journey, which we made in a post-chaise, a veritable journey of the good old times. The thought of them brought many an amusing remembrance to my uncle; but those which were most charming to him were his vacations passed at Trouville, then but a simple fishing village.

He met there some English people, the family of Admiral Collier, all of whom were beautiful and intelligent. The oldest daughters, Gertrude and Henrietta, soon became the intimate friends of my uncle and my mother. Gertrude, now Madame Tennant, lately wrote me some pages about her youth. I translate the following lines:—

"Gustave Flaubert was then like a young Greek. In full adolescence, he was tall and thin, supple and graceful as an athlete, unconscious of the gifts that he possessed, physically and morally, caring little for the impression he produced and entirely indifferent to accepted form. His dress consisted of a red flannel shirt, great trousers of blue cloth, a scarf of the same color around his waist and a cap put on no matter how, or often bare-headed. When I spoke to him of fame, or of influence, as desirable things that I esteemed, he listened, smiled, and seemed superbly indifferent. He admired what was beautiful in nature, art and literature and lived for that, as he said, without any thought of the personal. He cared neither for glory nor for gain. Was it not enough that a thing was true and beautiful? His great joy was in finding something that he judged worthy of admiration. The charm of his society was in his enthusiasm for all that was noble; and the charm of his mind was its intense individuality. He hated all hypocrisy. What was lacking in his nature, was an interest in exterior and useful things. If any one happened to say that religion, politics, or business had as great an interest for them as literature or art, he would open his eyes in astonishment and pity. To be literary, an artist, that alone was worth living for."

It was at Trouville also that he met the musical editor, Maurice Schlesinger and his wife. Many faces remained engraved on his memory of his sojourns by the sea, among others that of an old sailor, Captain Barbet and his little daughter, Barbette, a little hump-back always crying out to her dolls. Then there was Doctor Billard, and Father Couillère, mayor of the commune, at whose house they had repasts that lasted for six hours. He recalled these years in writing *A Simple Soul*. Madame Aubin, her two children, the house where she lived, and all the details so true, so appreciative, in this simple history, are of striking exactness. Madame was an aunt to my grandmother; Félicité and her parrot once lived.

In his last years, my uncle had an extreme desire to revive his youth. He wrote *A Simple Soul*, after his mother's death, to try to accomplish this. In painting the town where she was born, the hearth before which she had played, his cousins, the companions of his childhood, he found satisfaction, and that pleasure has brought from his pen his most touching pages, those perhaps where he allows us to divine most clearly the man under the writer. Recall that scene where Madame Aubin and her servant are arranging the trifling possessions that had belonged to Virginia. A large hat of black straw which my grandmother had worn awoke in my uncle a similar emotion. He would take that relic from the nail, look at it in silence, with eyes moistening, and then respectfully replace it.

Finally, the happy time of leaving college arrived, but the terrible question of choosing a profession, or taking up some career poisoned his joy. As a vocation, he cared only for literature, and "literature" is not a career; it leads to no "position." My grandfather wished his son to be a savant and a law practitioner. To devote himself to the unique and exclusive research for beauty of literary form, seemed to him almost folly. A man of character, eminently strong, and of very active habits, he comprehended with difficulty the nervous and somewhat feminine side which characterises all artistic organisations. With his mother my uncle found more encouragement, but she held to the point that he should obey his father, and he was resolved that Gustave should make his way in Paris. He set out, sad at leaving his own people, his sister especially.

At Paris he lived in the Rue de l'Est in a little bachelor apartment where he found himself badly installed. The noisy, free and easy pleasures of his comrades seemed to him stupid, so that he scarcely ever participated in them. He would remain alone, open one of his law books, which he would immediately put away, then extending himself upon his bed, he would smoke and dream for hours. He became very weary of this life, and grew sombre.

Pradier's studio alone put warmth in him again; he saw there all the artists of the day, and in contact with them he felt his instincts grow. One day he met Victor Hugo there. Some women visited the studio; it was there he met Louise Colet. He often went to see the pretty English girls of Trouville, to the salon of the editor, Maurice Schlesinger, and to the hospitable house of his father's friend, Doctor Jules Cloquet, who led him away one summer to the Pyrenees and to Corsica. The *Education Sentimental* was composed in remembrance of this epoch.

But in spite of friendship,—doubtless in spite of love,—a weariness without bounds invaded him. His work, which was contrary to his taste, became intolerable to him, his health was seriously affected and he returned to Rouen.

My mother's marriage, her death the year following, and a little later that of my grandfather, left my grandmother in such grief that she was happy to keep her son near her. Paris and the Law School were abandoned. It was then that, in company with Maxime Ducamp, he made the journey through Brittany and they wrote together the book: *Over Strand and Field. (A travers les Champs et les Grèves.)*

Upon his return, he began his *Saint Antoine,* his first great work. It had been preceded by many, of which fragments have been published since his death. The *Saint Antoine* composed then, was not the first known to the public. This work was undertaken at three different times before it was finally finished.

In 1849 Gustave Flaubert took a second journey
with Maxime Ducamp.   This time the two friends
directed their steps towards the Orient, which had
for so long been their dream!

## II.

My personal reminiscences date from his return.
He came back at evening; I was in bed, but they
awakened me.   He came to my little bed, raised me
suddenly and found me very droll in my long night-
gown; I remember that it extended far below my
feet.  He began to laugh very hard and then to imprint great kisses on my cheeks which made me
cry; I felt the cold of his moustache, humid with
dew, and was very glad when he put me down
again.  I was then five years old and we were at
the grandparents' house at Nogent.   Three months
later I saw him again in England, as I still remember
distinctly.   It was at the time of the first Exposition
at London.   They took me there and the crowd
frightened me; my uncle took me on his shoulder,
and I traversed the galleries overlooking everybody,
this time happy to be in his arms.   They chose me
a governess and we returned to Croisset.

My uncle wished to begin my education immediately.   The governess was to teach me only English;
my grandmother would teach me to read and write,
and for him was reserved history and geography.
He believed it useless to study grammar, holding that
it taught itself in reading, and that it was bad to
charge the memory of a young child with abstrac-

tions, which one begins where often they ought to finish.

Then began some years when we were all together.

Croisset, where we lived, is the first village on the bank of the Seine in going from Rouen to Havre. The house, long and low in shape, all white, must have been built about two hundred years. It had belonged to the monks of the Abbey of Saint-Ouen whom it served for a country house, and it pleased my uncle to think that Prévost had composed *Manon Lescaut* here.

In the interior court, where still remained the pointed roof and the guillotine-shaped windows of the seventeenth century, the construction was interesting, but the façade was ugly. It had undergone one of those remodellings in bad taste that were seen so often in the first Empire and the reign of Louis Philippe, at the beginning of the century. Above the entrance, after the fashion of bas-reliefs, were some villainous casts,—the seasons of Bouchardon — and the mantelpiece in the salon had on each side a representation of a mummy in white marble, a souvenir of the Egyptian country.

The rooms were few, but sufficiently large. The spacious dining-room, which occupied the centre of the house on the ground floor, opened upon the garden by a glass door flanked by two windows in full view of the river. It was pleasing and gay.

On the next story, at the right, a long corridor separated the chambers, and on the left was my uncle's study, or work-room. It was a large apartment, with a very low ceiling, but very light, because of five windows, of which three looked upon the whole length of the garden, the other two being in the front of the house. There was a pretty view of the turf, the beds full of flowers, the trees on the long terrace, and the Seine enframed in the foliage of a splendid tulip tree.

The ways of the house were subordinated to the taste of my uncle, my grandmother having, so to speak, no longer any personal life; she lived for the happiness of others. Her tenderness was in alarm at the slightest symptom of suffering which she thought she detected in her son, and she sought to envelop him in a calm atmosphere. In the morning she was on the defence against the least noise; towards ten o'clock the violent ringing of a bell would be heard, and some one would go to my uncle's room; not until then did every one awake. The domestic carried him his letters and newspapers, deposited on the night table a glass of fresh water and a well-filled pipe; then he opened the shutters, and the light streamed in. My uncle would seize his letters, run over the addresses, but rarely did he open one before taking a few whiffs from his pipe; then, having read them all, he would tap the neighbouring wall to call his mother, who would run in immediately and seat herself near his bed until he was ready to rise.

He made his toilet slowly, sometimes interrupting himself to go to the table and re-read some passage with which he was preoccupied. Although little complicated, his dress was not lacking in care, and his neatness expressed his refinement.

At eleven he came down to breakfast, where my grandmother, uncle Parain, the governess and I, were already assembled. We all loved uncle Parain infinitely. He had married my grandfather's sister and passed a great part of the year with us. At this time my uncle ate little, especially in the morning, finding that too much nourishment made him heavy and unfit for work. Almost never did he eat meat; only eggs, vegetables, a piece of cheese, fruit and a cup of cold chocolate. At dessert, he would relight his pipe — a little clay pipe — get up and go into the garden, where we followed. His favourite walk was the terrace walled in and bordered on one side by old willows cut straight across like a gigantic wall. This led to a little pavilion in the style of Louis XV., whose windows looked out upon the Seine. Very often on summer evenings we would all seat ourselves here under the balcony of graceful fretwork and remain for some calm hours, chatting together; the night would come, little by little, the last passers disappear; in the water opposite we could just distinguish the silhouette of a horse drawing a boat which glided along without noise; then the moon would begin to shine with a thousand sparkling rays, like a fine diamond powder, scintillating at our feet, while a light tug and two or three barques would slip from their moorings and invade the river. These belonged to the eel fishers who were starting at this time to set their nets.

My grandmother, who was very delicate, would cough, and my uncle would say: "It is time to return to the Bovary." The Bovary? What was that? I knew not. But I respected the name, those two words, as I respected everything that came from my uncle, and believed vaguely that it was a synonym for work, and work was writing, as was well understood. In fact, it was during these years, from 1852 to 1856 that he composed this novel.

We were rarely in the pavilion after breakfast. Fleeing from the midday sun, we mounted to a spot called "The Mercury," because of a statue of that god which formerly ornamented it. It was a second avenue situated above the terrace, which led to a charming shady footpath; some old yew-trees came out of the rocks in queer shapes, showing their bare roots and jagged trunks; they appeared to be suspended, holding only to the crumbling wall at the side by their roots. Above the alley was a kind of round-point, a circular bench concealed under some huge chestnut-trees. Through the branches one could see the tranquil waters and above them a large expanse of sky.

From time to time, a cloud would rapidly go by and vanish. It was the smoke of a steamboat; and immediately would appear between the interlaced branches the pointed masts of ships which were being towed to Rouen. Sometimes there would be seven, or nine. Nothing is more majestic and beautiful than the pomp of these floating houses, which suggest a far-off country. About one o'clock could be heard a sharp whistle; it was "the steamer," as they say in the country. Three times a day this boat crossed between Rouen and Bouille. The whistle was the signal of departure.

"Come," my uncle would say, "come to your lesson, my Caro;" and dragging me along, we would both go into his large study, where the shutters were carefully closed to keep out the heat. It was pleasant there; one breathed an odour of Oriental joss-sticks mingled with that of tobacco, also with perfumes that were wafted in through the door of his dressing-room. With a bound I would throw myself upon the great white bear-skin, which I adored, and cover his great head with kisses. My uncle, meantime, would be putting his pipe on the chimney-piece; and, selecting another, would fill it, light it, and seat himself in his leather armchair at the end of the room; he would cross one leg over the other, turn his back, take a file and begin to polish his nails, saying: "Let us see, where were you? Now, what do you remember from yesterday?"

"Oh! I know the history of Pelopidas and Epaminondas very well."

"Relate it, then."

I began, but naturally I became confused or I had forgotten.

"I am going to tell it to you once more," he would finally say.

Then I would approach and sit facing him on a long chair or upon the divan. I listened with a palpitating interest to the recitals that he made so amusing to me.

It was thus I learned all my ancient history, coming to the facts one after another, making reflections within my power, but remaining truly and profoundly observant; mature minds would have been able to listen without finding anything puerile in his teaching.

Sometimes I would stop him and ask: "Was he good?" And this question, applied to such men as Cambyses, Alexander or Alcibiades, was somewhat embarrassing for him to answer.

"Good?" he would say, "Yes . . . these were not very proper gentlemen, but . . . that is not the point."

But I was not satisfied, and I found that "my old boy," as I called him, knew even the smallest details of the people we were studying about.

The history lesson finished, we passed on to geography. He never wished me to study from a book. "Images, as many as possible," he said, "are the best means of learning in childhood." We had charts, spheres, games of patience which we could make and unmake together; then, to explain the difference between islands, peninsulas, bays, gulfs and promontories he would take a shovel and a pail of water and, in a little walk in the garden, make models of these in nature.

As I grew older, the lessons became longer and more serious. He continued them up to my seventeenth year, until my marriage. When I was ten years old, he obliged me to take notes while he was speaking, and when my mind was capable of comprehending it, he began to make me notice the artistic side of things, especially in my reading.

He considered no book dangerous that was well written; he held this opinion because of his intimate union of foundation and form: anything well written could not be badly thought out or basely conceived. It was not the crude detail, the raw fact that was pernicious or harmful, or likely to soil the intelligence; all that is in nature. There is nothing moral or immoral but the soul of him who represents nature, rendering it grand, beautiful, serene, small, ignoble, or tormenting. Such a thing as an obscene book well written could not exist, according to him.

Certainly he was very liberal in the reading he recommended to me, yet he was decided in allowing me nothing for amusement alone, and never would permit me to leave a book unfinished. "Continue to read the history of the Conquest," he wrote me, "and do not allow yourself to begin books and then leave them for some time. When one undertakes to read a book, it should be finished at a single blow. It is the only way of seeing it as a whole and of deriving any profit from it. Accustom yourself to following this idea. Since you are my pupil, I do not wish you to have that disconnected way of thinking, a mind unable to follow out anything, which is the attribute of persons of your sex."

He held to this intellectual discipline, judging it to be very useful. His teaching sought to impress itself upon my mind in the strongest manner possible. So easy in some ways, he was very rigorous on certain points; thus, he wished that the virtue of a woman consisted not alone of purity of morals, but that she might add that to what is exacted in an honest man.

My lesson finished, my uncle would seat himself at his table in his high-back, oak armchair and there remain until seven o'clock, allowing himself only a moment from time to time, to go to his window and breathe large whiffs of air. Then we dined, and chatted together awhile, as after breakfast. At nine o'clock, or ten at the latest, he would again take up his work with zeal, prolonging it far into the night. He was never more in the spirit of it than in these solitary hours when no sound could come to trouble him.

He remained thus many months in succession, seeing no one but Louis Bouilhet, his intimate friend, who came each Sunday, staying until Monday morning. A part of the night was passed in reading the work of the week. What delightful hours of expansion! There were loud cries of exclamation without end, some controversy over rejecting or keeping some epithet, or some reciprocal enthusiasm!

Three or four times a year, my uncle would go to Paris to pass some days at the house of the Helder's. All his distractions were limited to short absences. However, in 1856, having decided to publish *Madame Bovary*, he went to live at No. 42 Boulevard du Temple, in a house belonging to M. Mourier, director of the theatre of the *Délassements-Comiques*. Bouilhet was presenting his first piece, *Madame de Montarcy*, at the Odéon that year. He had already preceded his friend, left Rouen and his profession as tutor to live entirely by letters. My grandmother was not long in joining them; she spent some of the winter months in a furnished apartment, and two years later installed herself in the same house with her son, on the story above.

Although living so near, we were very independent. My uncle had taken into his service a valet named Narcisse, the queerest individual possible; he had been a domestic in my grandfather's house, and his drollery as well as his zeal prompted my uncle to engage him. Narcisse, an established farmer, married, and the father of six children, had left his wife and family with the greatest eagerness to follow the son of his old master for whom he had a respect amounting to fanaticism, but joined to that the greatest forgetfulness of difference in station. One day he returned completely drunk; my uncle perceived this and seated, or rather tumbled him into a chair in the kitchen. He aided him to reach his room, and to stretch himself out on the bed. Then Narcisse, in a supplicating air, said: "Ah! sir! complete your goodness by pulling off my boots." And this was done by the too indulgent master!

Our friends amused themselves with the reflections of this servant and his repartee; certain of them sent him their books. He was often found sitting in the study, or before a bookcase, with a feather duster under one arm and a book in his hand; he read in a high voice, imitating his master. But these artistic endeavours, joined to the abuse of small glasses, completely disordered the brain of the poor devil; and he was obliged to return to the fields.

During these winter months, I regretted the summer days because the great success of *Madame Bovary* followed by a famous lawsuit had given to my uncle a celebrity that made him sought after. He went out much and I saw less of him.

The apartment of the Boulevard du Temple blossomed on certain days. It was a pleasure to give little repasts there to our intimate friends; I remember those in which I took part and which had around the table Sainte-Beuve, Monsieur and Madame Sandeau, Monsieur and Madame Cornu, these last brought by Jules Duplan, the faithful friend of Gustave Flaubert; then Charles d'Osmoy, and Théophile Gautier came very often, and on Sundays the door was open wide and friends were numerous.

This epoch was for my uncle the beginning of relations which lasted until his death. He assiduously frequented the *salon* of the Princess Mathilde. He found gathered there scholars, artists, and some of his intimate friends; he relished strongly this intellectual and worldly life. He went also to the Tuileries and was invited to Compiègne; from his sojourn at the castle there came to him the thought of a great romance which should bring out the French and the Turkish civilisations.

Then he also had dinners at Magny which, in the beginning, numbered only half a score of people: Sainte-Beuve, Théophile Gautier, the two De Goncourts, Garvarni, Renan, Taine, the Marquis of Chennevières, Bouilhet and my uncle. Their conversations abounded in the highest interest.

Finally, the month of May arrived and we returned to the tranquil life at Croisset.

Beginning in 1860 to write *Salammbô,* my uncle soon perceived that a voyage to the site of what was once Carthage was necessary to him, and he set out for Tunis. On his return he accompanied his mother to Vichy. We went there the two years following.

My grandmother's health not permitting her to go out with me, my uncle took her place; he accompanied me in my walks and on Sunday even took me to church, in spite of the independence of his beliefs, or rather because of that independence. We often went when it was pleasant, and seated ourselves under the little white-leaved poplars along the main walk; he would read while I sketched, and interrupting his reading, he would speak to me of what it suggested to him, or begin to recite verse, or entire pages of prose which he knew by heart. What he most often recited was Montesquieu and Chateaubriand. His memory disclosed itself equally in dates or in historic facts. But let him recall some literary remembrance and he was truly surprising; in a volume read twenty years before he could name the page and the spot on the page which had pleased him; and, going straight to his library and opening the book, he would say: "Here it is," with a certain satisfaction which made the light shine in his eyes.

At Vichy he returned to old acquaintances: Doctor Villemain whom he met in Egypt, and Lambert Bey, one of the adepts of the *Père Enfantin.*

My marriage came in 1864, changing all our life. I lived a great part of the year at Neuville near Dieppe, going no oftener to Croisset than twice a year, in the spring and in the autumn. My uncle made only short visits at my house; any change of place troubling him extraordinarily and disturbing his work. It was necessary for him to work at an extreme tension, and it was impossible for him to find himself in this state elsewhere than at his great round table in his study, where he was sure that nothing would distract him. This love of tranquillity, which he carried later to an excess, had begun already to exercise a tyranny upon his least action. At the end of a few days, I could see that he was nervous and I felt that he was desirous of returning to his beloved labour.

For ten years our lives were less mingled, save for the month of April in 1871. When I returned from England where I had passed some months, I found him much changed. The war had made a profound impression upon him; his "old Latin blood" had revolted at this return to barbarity. Obliged to flee from his house,—for he would not for anything in the world be under the necessity of speaking to a Prussian,—he took refuge in Rouen in a little lodging near the Havre quay where he was badly housed. This seemed to be a bereavement; my grandmother, now aged, no longer occupied herself with the management of the household, and instead of transporting

their furniture and necessary objects from the country
to the town (and that would have been easy to do),
they left all at Croisset, where a score of men, officers
and soldiers, had established themselves.

The fatal lack of employment that a disturbed life
brings, the thought of his study, his books, his home
soiled by the presence of the enemy, brought to my
uncle's heart and mind frightful anxiety and grief.
The arts appeared to him dead. Why? Was it possible? Could it be that an intelligent country would
cause these billows of blood? But there were scholars
who were holding Paris in siege, and hurling project-
iles against the monuments!

He thought that he should return to his house to
find nothing there. He was deceived; save some
trifling objects without value, such as cards, a pen-
knife, or a paper-cutter, they had respected absolutely
all that belonged to him. One thing only about the
return was suffocating,—the odour of the Prussian,
as the French call it, an odour of greased boots.
The walls were impregnated with it, through their
stay there of three long months, and it was necessary
to paint and redecorate the rooms in order to get rid
of it.

Six months passed without my uncle being able to
write, and finally, he was at my house at Neuville
when, yielding to my supplications, he began again,
this time finishing *The Temptation of Saint Antony*.

There was in Gustave Flaubert's nature a sort of
impossibility of being happy, and a tendency continually to turn back in order to compare and analyse.
Even at the age of the most absolute joys, he dis-
sected them so that he saw nothing in them but the
skeleton of pleasure.

When, on descending the Nile, he wrote the pages entitled: *Au bord de la Cange,* he regretted his home on the banks of the Seine. The landscape under his eye never seemed to captivate him; it was later that he recalled it with pleasure, while man, with his foolishness, and his conversation, was intensely interesting to him. "Foolishness," he would say, "enters my pores." And when he was reproached for not going out more, or for remaining so much in the country, he would say indignantly: "But nature devours me! If I remain extended on the grass for a long time, I believe that I can feel the plants growing under my body"; and he would add: "You don't know what trouble confusion and change make me."

As to himself, in the most grievous events of his life he wrote down his sensations, seeking, scrutinising the most remote corners of his nature, however veiled or intimate. A fact in a newspaper, a droll story of people he knew, stupidities written by authoritative pens, the manifestation of their self-conceit or their greed, were to him so much subjects of experience that he recorded them and slipped them into his portfolio; he could not comprehend the art that sought only gain; according to him, mere money could not reward the artist; and between the five hundred francs which the editor Michael Lévy sent him for his five years' work on *Madame Bovary,* and the ten thousand francs which he received some years later for *Salammbô,* he saw very little difference.

In his note-books of travel in the Pyrenees at seventeen years of age, he pointed out the silliness of the reflections of travelers about Lake Gaube and the inn near Gavarnie. Even here is the beginning of the *Dictionary of Accepted Ideas by Bouvard and Pécuchet*. This strong sense of the comic was useful in opposition to his love for the ideal, as his love for farce corrected his inborn melancholy.

## III.

In 1875, the loss of a considerable sum of money changed our circumstances. My husband saw all that he had disappear in commercial transactions. Married under the dowry laws so common in Normandy, I could dispose of only a part of my property in his favour. My uncle made up the deficit with an entirely spontaneous generosity, giving all that he possessed to save our position. Nothing remained for him to live on except the interest that we had engaged to pay him, and the very mediocre revenue from his books. To sell Croisset was the thought which first presented itself to our minds; this property had been given me by my grandmother, with the expressed wish that her son Gustave should continue to live there. This consideration, added to my uncle's repugnance to separating himself from it, decided us in the resolution to keep it. Loneliness weighed upon his tender nature, and an arrangement of a life in common was agreeable to him. He passed the greater part of the time in the country; and, in Paris, having taken his apartment again in the Rue Murillo, we took one on the same landing, on the fifth floor of a house situated at the angle of the Rue du Faubourg-Saint-Honoré and the Avenue de la Reine-Hortense.

We were then together as formerly, and our confidential talks were more frequent, deeper and more intimate than those of my childhood's days. In the retired life that we led, my uncle spoke to me as to a friend; we talked on all subjects, but preferably those of literature, religion and philosophy, which we discussed without any anger or disagreeable results, although we were often of a different opinion.

It is easy to see that a man who could write *Saint Antoine* must be superabundantly occupied with religious thought as found in humanity, and its manifold manifestations. The old theogonies interested him extremely, and the excessive in all people had an infinite attraction for him. The anchorite, the recluse at the Thebans, provoked his admiration, and he felt towards them as towards the Bouddha on the bank of the Ganges. He often re-read his Bible. That verse of Isaiah: "How beautiful upon the mountains are the feet of him that bringeth good tidings!" he thought sublime. "Reflect, sift the thing to the bottom," he would say to me enthusiastically.

A pagan on his artistic side, he was, through the needs of his soul, pantheistic. Spinoza, whom he much admired, did not fail to leave his imprint upon him. Besides, no belief of his mind, save his belief in beauty, was so fixed that it was not capable of listening to the other side, and admitting even, up to a certain point, the obverse. He loved to repeat with Montaigne, what was perhaps the last word of his philosophy, that it is necessary to sleep upon the pillow of doubt.

But let us return to the work of the day. Here he is happy in reading to me the freshly hatched phrase that he has just finished; I assist, as a motionless witness, the slow creation of these pages so labouriously elaborated. In the evening, the same lamp lights us, I, seated beside the large table, where I am employed with my needlework, or in reading; he, struggling with his work. Bent forward, he writes feverishly, then turns his back upon his work, strikes his arms upon those of his chair and utters a groan, for a moment almost like a rattle in the throat; but suddenly his voice modulates sweetly, swelling proudly: he has found the desired expression and is repeating the phrase to himself. Then he gets up and walks around his study with long steps, scanning the syllables as he goes and is content; it is a moment of triumph after exhausting labour.

Having arrived at the end of a chapter, he would often give himself a day of rest in order to read over at his ease what he had written, to see the "effect." He read in a unique fashion, chanting and emphasising so much that at first it seemed exaggerated, but ending in a way that was very agreeable. It was not only his own works that he read in this way; from time to time he would give real literary sessions, becoming impassioned with the beauty that he found; and his enthusiasm was communicative, so that it was impossible to remain cold, or keep from vibrating with him.

Among the ancients, Homer and Æschylus were his gods. Aristophanes gave him more pleasure than Sophocles, Plautus than Horace, whose merit he thought over-praised. How many times have I heard him say that he would prefer above all things to be a comic poet!

Shakespeare, Byron, and Victor Hugo he profoundly admired, but he never comprehended Milton. He said: "Virgil has created the amorous woman, Shakespeare the amorous young girl; all others are more or less far-removed copies of Dido or Juliette."

In French prose he read again and again Rabelais and Montaigne, recommending them to all who wished to meddle with writing.

Literary enthusiasms had always existed in him; one that he loved to recall was that he experienced on his first reading of *Faust*. He read it on the eve of Easter as he was leaving college; instead of returning to his father's house, he found himself, not knowing how, in a spot called "Queen's walk." It is a beautiful promenade planted with high trees upon the left bank of the Seine, a little removed from the town. He was seated upon the steep bank; the clocks in the churches across the river resounded in the air and mingled with the poetry of Goethe. "Christ had arisen, peace and joy were complete. Announce then, deep bells, the beginning of the Easter day, celestial sounds, powerful and sweet! Why seek you me in the dust?" His head was turned and he came back like one lost in revery, scarcely realising things of earth.

How could this man, so great an admirer of the beautiful, find so much happiness in uncovering human turpitude, especially that found outside the realm of virtue? Must it not be from his worship of the true? His revelations seemed to be the confirmation of his philosophy and he rejoiced in them through love of that truth which he believed he was penetrating.

Numerous projects of work occupied his mind. He mentioned especially a story of the people of Thermopylæ that he intended to begin. He found that he had lost too much time in the preparatory research for his works and wished to employ the rest of his life in art, pure art. His belief in form would cross his mind; this caused him one day to cry out in his whimsical spontaneity: "I attach myself to the Ideal!" Then immediately laughing at our applause, he said: "Not bad, that! Poetry, isn't it? I begin to comprehend art."

A true artist, for him, never could be wicked, for an artist is before all an observer; the first quality for an observer is to possess good eyes. If they are blurred with passion, or personal interest, things escape them; a good heart makes a good mind!

His worship of the beautiful led him to say: "The moral is not only a part of the æsthetic, but its condition foundationally."

Two kinds of men were especially displeasing to him and were ever a subject for his disgust: the critic who never produced anything, but judges all things (to whom he preferred a candle merchant), and the educated gentleman who believes himself an artist, who has imagined Venice different from what it is, and has had disillusions. When he met a person of this kind, there was an explosion of scorn which showed itself, perhaps through cutting answers (he would pretend that he had no imagination, never fancied anything nor knew anything) or through a silence still more haughty.

Up to the time of his death, I had the advantage of continuing that serious, calm life from which my feminine mind had so much to gain. Many of my uncle's best friends were dead: Louis Bouilhet, Jules Duplan, Ernest Lemarié, Théophile Gautier, Jules de Goncourt, Ernest Feydeau, and Sainte-Beuve, while others were far away. His meetings with Maxime Ducamp were only rare; from 1852 the two friends no longer followed the same routes, as their correspondence witnesses.

In friendship my uncle was perfect; of a devotion absolutely faithful, without envy, happier in the success of a friend than in his own; but he brought into his friendly relations some exactions that those who were the object of them found it difficult to support. The heart that was bound to him by a common love of art (and all his deep attachments were upon this basis) should belong to him without reserve.

Wherefore, five years before his death, he received this short note in response to a package containing his *Three Stories :—*

"My Dear Friend: I thank you for your volume. I have not read any of it, for I am absolutely besotted by the finishing of a work of mine. I should have it done in eight or ten days and I shall then reward myself by reading you. Yours,       Maxime Ducamp."

His heart suffered and recoiled on itself bitterly. Where now was the ardent desire of knowing quickly the thought that springs from the brain of a friend? Where were those beautiful years of youth? where was the faith in each other?

Nevertheless, there were still some natures that he loved much. Among the young, in the first rank, was the nephew of Alfred Le Poittevin, Guy de Maupassant, his "disciple," as he loved to call him. Then, his friendship with George Sand was for his mind no less than for his heart, a great comfort. But of his own generation, he often said that only Edmond de Goncourt and Ivan Tourgenief remained;

with them he tasted the full joy of æsthetic conversation. Alas! they became more and more rare, these hours of intimate talks, because, for this overflow of soul it was necessary to find minds taken up with the same things, and the sojourns in Paris became farther and farther apart. His solitude, always terrible, became unbearable when I was not there, and often, to escape it, he would call on the old nurse of his childhood. At her fireside his heart would become warm again. In a letter to me he said: "To-day I have had an exquisite conversation with 'Mademoiselle Julie.' In speaking of the old times, she brought before me a crowd of portraits and images which expanded my heart. It was like a whiff of fresh air. She has (in language) an expression of which I shall make use. It was in speaking of a lady, 'She was very fragile,' she said, 'thundering so!' *Thundering* after *fragile* is full of depth! Then we spoke of Marmontel and of the *New Heloise,* something that could not be done among ladies nor scarcely among gentlemen."

When he was much alone, he would sometimes take up his love of nature, which would relieve him from his work for a moment. "Yesterday," he wrote, "in order to refresh my poor noddle, I took a walk to Canteleu. After travelling for two solid hours, Monsieur took a chop at Pasquet's, where they were making ready for New Year's Day. Pasquet showed a great joy at seeing me, because I recalled to him 'that poor Monsieur Bouilhet'; and he sighed many times. The weather was so beautiful, the moon so bright in the evening that I went out to walk again at ten o'clock in the garden, 'under the glimmer of the stars of night.' You cannot imagine what a lover of nature I have become; I look at the sky, the trees and the verdure with a pleasure I never knew before. I could wish to be a cow that I might eat grass."

But he would seat himself again at his table and let many months slip by without being seized with the same desire.

At the beginning of the year 1874, he began *Bouvard and Pécuchet,* a subject which had interested him for thirty years. He intended it at first to be very short—a novel of about forty pages. Here is how the idea came to him: Seated with Bouilhet on a bench of the Boulevard at Rouen, opposite the asylum for the aged, they amused themselves by dreaming of what they should be some day; and, having begun gaily the supposed romance of their existence, suddenly they cried: "And who knows? we may finish, perhaps, like these old decrepits in this asylum." Then they began to imagine the friendship of two clerks, their life, their retiring from business, etc., etc., in order finally to finish their days in misery. These two clerks became "Bouvard and Pécuchet." This romance, so difficult of execution, discouraged my uncle at more than one undertaking. He was even obliged to lay it aside and go to Concarneau to join his friend George Pouchet, the naturalist.

Down there, on the Brittany strand, he began the legend of *Saint Julian the Hospitaller,* which was immediately followed by *A Simple Soul* and *Hérodias.* He wrote these three stories rapidly and then took up *Bouvard and Pécuchet* again, a heavy care, under which he must die.

Few existences bear witness to unity so complete as his: his letters show that at nine years of age he was preoccupied with art as if he were fifty. His life, as has been stated by all those who have spoken about him, was, from the awakening of his intelligence to the day of his death, the long development of the same passion — Literature. He sacrificed all to that; his love and tenderness were never separated from his art. Did he regret in the last years of his life that he had not followed the common route? Some words which came from his lips one day when we were walking beside the Seine made me think so: we had just visited one of my friends whom we had found among her charming children. "They are in the right," he said to me, alluding to that household of the honest and good family; "Yes," he repeated to himself, gravely, "they are in the right." I did not trouble his thoughts, but remained silent by his side. This walk was one of our last.

Death took him in full health. It was at evening, and his letter was all good cheer, expressing the joy he felt at seeing himself confirmed in a conjecture that he had made regarding a plant. He had written me these interesting lines upon his work, of which only a few pages remained: "I am right! I have the assurance of the Professor of Botany in the *Jardin des Plantes,* and I was right; because the æsthetic is true, and to a certain intellectual degree (when one has some method) one is not deceived; the reality does not yield to the ideal, but confirms it. It has been necessary for me to make three journeys into different regions for *Bouvard and Pécuchet* before finding their setting, that best fit for action. Ah! ha! I have triumphed! I flatter myself it is a success!"

He had made arrangements to set out for Paris to join me again. It was the day of his departure, he was coming from the bath and mounting to his study; the cook was going up to serve his breakfast, when she heard him call and hastened to him. Already his tense fingers could not loosen a bottle of salts which he held in his hand. He tried to utter some words that were unintelligible in which she could distinguish: "Eylau — go — bring — avenue — I know him — "

A letter received from me that morning had told him that Victor Hugo was going to live in the Avenue d'Eylau; it was without doubt a remembrance of this news that he had in mind, as well as an appeal for help. He was cared for by his neighbor and friend, Doctor Fortin.

The last glimmer of his thought evoked the great poet who had caused his whole nature to vibrate. Immediately he fell into unconsciousness. Some moments later they found that he no longer breathed. Apoplexy had been the thunderbolt.

CAROLINE COMMANVILLE.

PARIS, *December, 1886.*

# CORRESPONDENCE.

## TO MADAME X.

CROISSET,
*Monday Night, June,* 1853.

EELING myself in a grand humor of style this morning, after giving my niece her lesson in geography, I seized upon my *Bovary,* sketching three pages in the afternoon which I have just rewritten this evening. Its movement is furious and full, and I shall doubtless discover a thousand repetitions which it will be necessary to strike out as soon as I come to look it over a little. What a miracle it would be for me to write even two pages in a day, when heretofore I have scarcely been able to write three in a week! With the *Saint Antony* that was, indeed, the way I worked, but I can no longer content myself with that. I wish *Bovary* to be at the same time heavier and more flowing. I believe that this week will see me well advanced, and that in about a fortnight I shall be able to read Bouilhet the whole of the beginning (a hundred and twenty pages), which, if it goes well, would be a great encouragement, and I shall have passed if not the most difficult part at least the

most annoying. But there are so many delays! I am
not yet at the point where I can credit our last interview at Mantes. What foolish and severe vexation you
must have passed through that week, my poor friend!
About cases like M ——, who throw themselves at your
feet, the best thing to do is to pass the sponge over
them immediately; but if you would care the least
bit in the world for the elder Lacroix or the great
Sainte-Beuve to receive something on the face or elsewhere, you have only to tell me and it is a commis-
sion of which I shall acquit myself with despatch on
my next visit to Paris, in the old-time manner between two journeys; but could you not show Lacroix
the door with a single word? What good is there
in discussing, replying to, and angering him? This is
all very easy to say in cold blood, is it not? It is
always this accursed passion element which causes us
all our annoyances. How true is Larochefoucauld's remark: "The virtuous man is he who allows himself
to be concerned with nothing." Yes, it is necessary
to bridle the heart, to hold it in leash like an enraged
bulldog, and then let it loose at a bound at the op-
portune moment. Run, run, my old fellow, bark
loudly and go at top speed; what these rogues have
that is superior to us is patience. So in this story,
Lacroix by his cowardly tenacity wearies De Lisle,
who ends by becoming vexed and leaving the game
and *Le Jeune irrité* (the whole of Sainte-Beuve is
in these words) will not have had finally either a
sword in his paunch or a foot to his coat-tails, and
will privately begin his machinations anew, as Homais
would say.

You are astonished to find yourself the butt of so
much calumny, opposition, indifference and ill-will.

You will be more so and have more of it; it is
the reward of the good and the beautiful: one may
calculate the value of a man from the number of
his enemies and the importance of a work by the
evil said of it. Critics are like fleas which always
jump upon white linen and adore lace. That re-
proach sent by Sainte-Beuve to the *Paysanne* estab-
lishes my belief in the *Paysanne* more firmly than
Victor Hugo's praise of it; we give our praise to
everybody, but our blame, no! Who is there that
has not made a parody on the mediocre?

In regard to Hugo, I do not believe that it is
time to write to him; you gave him a month for an
answer, and it is not more than two weeks since
our packet left; so it is necessary to wait at least
as long as that, provided it has not been seized.
Every precaution was taken, my mother addressing
the letter herself.

What can this phrase in your letter this morning
mean in speaking of De Lisle? "I believe that I was
deceived in my impression of yesterday." The words
of the *bourgeois* at Préault are good. Have I told
you what a curate of Trouville said one day after I
had dined with him? When I refused champagne (I
had already eaten and drunk enough to make me
fall under the table), my curate was astonished and
turned on me an eye! such an eye! an eye express-
ing envy, admiration, and disdain together, and said
to me, shrugging his shoulders: "Come, now! all
you young people from Paris who *gulp down champagne* with your fine suppers, make very little
mouths when you come to the provinces!" And it
was so easy to understand that between the words
"fine suppers" and "gulp" he meant to say "with

the actresses!" What horizons! and to know that I
excited this brave man! In this connection I am
going to allow myself a quotation: "Come now!"
said the chemist, shrugging his shoulders, "do you
know about these fine parties at the house of the
traitor! the masked balls! the champagne? All this
goes on, I assure you."

"I do not believe that it injures him," objected
Bovary.

"Nor I either," quickly replied M. Homais, "and it
may be necessary for him to keep them up or be
taken for a Jesuit. But if you only knew what
lives those fellows lead, in the Latin Quarter with
their actresses! Generally speaking, students are well
looked upon in Paris. For the little attractiveness
that they have, they are received into the best society, and there are even ladies of the Faubourg
Saint-Germain who fall in love with them and, in
consequence sometimes give them opportunities of
making fine marriages." In two pages I believe I
have collected all the stupidity that one hears in the
provinces about Paris,—student life, actresses, the
pickpockets you encounter in the public gardens, and
the cooking at the restaurants, "always more un-
wholesome than provincial cooking."

That stiffness of which Préault accuses me is
astonishing; it appears that when I have on a black
coat, I am not the same man. And it is certain that
I am then wearing a kind of disguise which my face
and manners ought to resent, so much effect has the
exterior upon the interior. It is the cap that moulds
the head, and all troopers have about them the imbecile stiffness of hard lines. Bouilhet pretends that,
out in the world, I have the air of a drilled, *bourgeois*

officer. Is it on this account that the illustrious Turgan calls me "the major?" He also maintains that I have a military air, and one could pay me no compliment that would be less agreeable. If Préault knew me, he would, on the contrary, find that I have a too bare-breasted air like the good captain; but how beautiful Ferrat must have been with his "good southern fury;" I can see him there now gasconading; it is tremendous. And, speaking of the grotesque, I was overwhelmed at the funeral of Madame Pouchet; decidedly, the good God is romantic, for he continually mingles the two kinds together. Nevertheless, while I was looking at the poor Pouchet, who was in torture, shaking like a reed in the wind, do you know what came up before me? A gentleman who asked me, on my voyage: "What kind of museums have they in Egypt? *What is the condition of their public libraries?*" And when I demolished his illusions, he was desolate. "Is it possible!" said he. "What an unfortunate country! What a civilization!" etc. . . .

The burial was Protestant, the priest speaking in French beside the grave; Monsieur would prefer it so . . . "since Catholicism is denuded of the flowers of rhetoric." O humans! O mortals! and to think we are always duped, that we have the vanity to believe ourselves imaginative, when the reality crushes us! I went to that ceremony with the intention of elevating my mind to the point of penetration; to try to discover a few pebbles; and then—these blocks fell upon my head! The grotesque deafened my ears, and the pathetic was in convulsions before my eyes. Whence I draw (or rather withdraw) this conclusion: *It is never necessary to fear exaggerating;*

all the great ones have done it: Michael-Angelo, Rabelais, Shakespeare and Molière. It is a question of making a man take an injection when he has no syringe; well, we must fill the theatre with apothecaries' syringes; that is clearly the way to reach genius in its true centre, which is very ridiculous. But to suppress exaggeration, there must be continuity, proportion, and harmony in itself. If your good men have a hundred feet, your mountains should be twenty miles high; and what is the ideal if it is not a magnifying?

Adieu; work well, see only friends, mount to the ivory tower, and let come what may.

## TO MADAME X.

CROISSET, *Saturday night.*

FINALLY I have finished my first part (of the second part); that is, I am at the point where I had intended to be at our last interview at Mantes; you see how great a delay this is! I shall pass still another week in re-reading all this and copying it, and a week from to-morrow I shall spout it to my lord Bouilhet. If this goes, a great anxiety will be removed, at least, and one good thing I can be sure of, that the foundation is well established; but I think however, that this book will have one great fault: that is, the fault of material proportion. I have already two hundred and sixty pages which contain only the preparation for action, some expositions, more or less disguised, of character (it is true that they are graduated), and of landscapes and places. My conclusion, which will be the recital of the death of my little woman, her funeral, and the sorrow of the husband, will follow with sixty pages at least. There remains, then, for the body of the action one hundred and twenty, or one hundred and sixty pages at the most. Is this not a great defect? What reassures me (in a slight degree), however, is that this book is a biography rather than a gradual development. The drama is a small part of it, so the dramatic element is well drowned in the general tone of the book; perhaps it will not be noticed that there is a want of harmony between the different phases so much as in their development; and then, it seems to me that life itself is a little like this. Our passions are like volcanoes; they grumble continually, but the eruption is only intermittent.

Unfortunately, the French mind has such a rage for amusement, it is necessary for it always to be seeing things! It cares so little for that which is poetry for me, or for knowing the *exposition,* that perhaps, as one may strike it picturesquely through tableaux, or morally through psychological analysis, it may serve exceedingly well that I wear a blouse, or have the appearance of doing so.

This is not the only day that I have suffered from writing in this language and thinking in it! At bottom I am German! The force of study has rubbed off all my southern mists. I wish to make books where only phrases are written (if one may so put it), as one lives by breathing only air; what vexes me is the trickery of the plan, the combinations for effect, and all the calculations which are the art of it, and upon which the effect of style depends exclusively.

And you, good muse, dear colleague in all (colleague comes from *colligere,* to bind together), have you worked well this week? I am curious to see that second recital. I have to recommend only two things: First, follow your metaphors closely; second, no details outside the subject; work in a straight line. *Parbleu!* We shall make some arabesques when we wish to, and better than anybody's. We must show the classicists that we are more classic than they, and make the romanticists turn pale with rage by surpassing their attempts. I believe the thing feasible, although of no importance. When a verse is good, it loses its school. A good verse by Boileau resembles a good verse by Hugo. Perfection has everywhere the same character, which is precision and justness.

If the book I am writing with so much trouble comes to any good, I shall have established two truths by its execution alone, which are for me axioms of knowledge: first, that poesy is purely subjective, that there are not in literature beautiful art subjects, and that Yvetot is worth as much as Constantinople; consequently, one may write one thing as well as another, it matters not what. The artist must raise all; he is like a pump, having in him a great duct which descends to the entrails of things, to the deepest stratum, and makes leap into the light, in giant jets, what was under the earth and seen by no one but himself.

Shall I have a letter from you on awakening? Your letters have not been numerous this week, my friend! But I suppose it is work which has kept you.

What an admirable face Father Babinet, member of the reading committee of the Odéon, will have! I can see now his *facies,* as my chemist would say, listening to the pieces as they are read.

There is taking place here an interesting case. A judge of the court of assizes, a brave man, is accused of killing his wife and then, having sewed her in a sack, of throwing her into the water. This poor woman had many lovers, and some one discovered at her house (it was a workman of the lowest class) a portrait and a letter from a gentleman, a chevalier of the Legion of Honor, a rallying Legitimist, Member of the General Council, of the Building Associations, etc., . . . of all the Associations, well known among the vestry, member of the Society of Saint-Vincent de Paul, of the Society of Saint-Regis, of the Children's Society, and all the humbugs possible; highly placed in fine society of the right kind, one of those persons who are an honour to a country and of whom it is said: "We are happy to possess such a gentleman"; and here, at a blow, it is discovered that this merry fellow has been carrying on relations (this is the phrase) with this merry lass — relations of the most disgusting kind, yes, Madame! Ah! great Heavens! I jeer like a beggar when I see all those fine people in the hands of the law; the humiliations these good gentlemen receive (they who find honours everywhere) seem to me to be the just punishment of their false pride. It is a disgrace to be always wishing to shine; it is debasing to mount to the heights and then sink into the mire with the mob! One should keep his level. And while there is not in my make-up much liking for democracy, I nevertheless love what is common, even ignoble, when it

is sincere.   But that which lies, which poses, which
affects  a  condemnation  of  passion  and  assumes  a
grimace of virtue, revolts me beyond all limits.  I feel
now  for  my  kind  a  serene  hatred,  or  an  inactive  pity
which is akin to it.   I have  made  great  progress  in
two years, and the political state of things has confirmed  my  old  theories  à  *priori,*  upon  the  biped
without feathers, whom all in all I consider a turkey
and a vulture.

Adieu, dear dove.


TO  MADAME  X.

CROISSET,  *Tuesday,*  1  *A.  M.*

I  AM  overwhelmed;  my  brain  is  dancing  in  my
head.   I  have  been  since  six  o'clock  this  evening
until  now  recopying  seventy-seven  successive  pages,
and  now  they  make  but  fifty-three.   It is torture.  The
ramifications  of  my  vertebræ  to  the  neck,  as  M.
Enault  remarks,  are  broken  from  having  bent  my
head so long.   What with the repetition of words, the
*alls,* the *buts,* the *fors* and the *howevers* I had to
strike out, there is never any end to it, which is the
way  with  this  diabolical  prose.   There  are,  nevertheless,  good  pages,  and  I  believe  that,  as  a  whole,  it
moves along; but I doubt if I shall  be ready to read
it all to Bouilhet on Sunday.  Just think! since the end
of February, I have written fifty-three pages!  What
a  charming  profession!   It  is  like  whipping  cream
when one would like to be rolling marbles.

I  am  very  tired,  but  have,  however,  many  things
to  say.   I  have  just  written  four  lines  to  Ducamp,

not for you; that would have been a reason for his showing you more malevolence — I know the man. This is the reason why I wrote him: to-day I received the last package of his photographs, of which I had never spoken to him, and the note was to thank him for it. That was all; I said nothing further. If, in the article on the philosophers, on Wednesday, he uses your name accompanied with any harmful allusions, I will do what you wish; but for my part, I should propose to break off squarely in a pretty, well-defined letter. However, do not let us torment ourselves, since the thing will doubtless not take place. It is Bouilhet's opinion (my note to-day is from a contrary hypothesis) that it is best to be on good terms when the rupture comes and be able to say to him: here is still another time that you are disobliging to me; good evening and good-bye. Do you understand?

As for Enault's article, it seems to me, good Muse, as if you had exaggerated it. It is stupid and foolish and all that, with its *feminosities,* "sensible woman," "younger woman," etc.— which have evidently come from Madame ——, who is jealous of you from all reports, and on that I would bet my head. It is our opinion, both Bouilhet's and mine, that he labours hard over his little monthly billets without ever saying anything. Bouilhet is profoundly indignant and proposes not even going to see him when he next goes to Paris; but what difference does it make to us, the opinion of my lord Enault, either written or spoken? As Ducamp said to Ferrat: Can you expect, in the midst of the whirlwind in which he lives, with his fascinating personality, his officer's badge, his receptions at the house of M. de Persigny, etc., that he could preserve enough perspi-

cacity to feel a new, original, or novel thing? Besides, in this arrangement, there may be something
agreed upon. We never can turn a negro white and
we never can hinder the mediocre from being mediocre. I assure you that if he were to say to me
"I have had curvature of the spine or softening of
the brain," it would make me laugh. Do you know
what I found out to-day from his photographs? The
only one he did not publish was the one represent-
ing our hotel at Cairo and the garden before our
windows where I stood in Nubian costume; it is a
bit of malice on his part. He wishes that I did not
exist; I have weighed him, as have you and every
body else. The work is dedicated to Cormenin, with
a dedicatory epigraph in Latin, and in the text is an
epigraph taken from Homer, all in Greek. The good
Maxime does not know a declension, but that does
not matter. He has had the German work of Leip-
sius translated and has pillaged it impudently (in the
text that I looked over) without quoting it once. I
heard that from a friend of his that I met on the
train; you know I said he must have pillaged it, for
there were all sorts of inscriptions that he never
would have valued, which are not in the books that
we meet in our travels, but which he reports as having been appreciated by him; it is like all the rest
of his work. As for the *Paysanne,* the eulogy which
Bouilhet wrote him about it (at the same time he
wrote to De Lisle, a letter which has met with no response) is the cause, you may be sure, of his remark
to Ferrat. Finally, all that is of very little importance. Still, we have been very much vexed all Sunday afternoon from it, these stories demoralising lord
Bouilhet a little, in which respect I find him weak,

and me also, for I am caught in it. Frankly now, it is stupid to permit these fellows to trouble us so. In fact, I find that in injuries, stupidities, foolishness, etc., it is necessary to be angry only when something is said to one's face. Make grimaces at my back as much as you wish, my breeches alone contemplate you.

I love you so much when I see you calm and know that you are working well, and still more, perhaps, when I know that you are suffering, for then you write me such superb letters, so full of fire. But, poor dear soul, take care of thyself, and tax only in moderation thy southern fury, as you called it in speaking of Ferrat.

The advice of De Lisle relative to the *Acropole* is good. First, send the manuscript to Villemain as you sent it to Jersey (I have received no letter about it, which seems strange, and my mother will write some day to Madame Farmer if I receive nothing); you could even make some corrections if you find it necessary although it seems good to me, except about the Barbarians, which I persist in finding much the weakest; second, try to have it appear in the *Press;* third, we shall find some plan, you may be sure. Bouilhet will be there this winter and he will aid you. His last fossil, the third piece, "Springtime," is superb; there is in it a pecking of birds around gigantic nests which is gigantic in itself. But he gets too sad, my poor Bouilhet; it is necessary to straighten up and em . . . humanity which em . . . us! Oh! I shall be avenged! In fifteen years from now I shall have undertaken a great modern romance where they shall all pass in review. I think that *Gil Blas* has perhaps done this, and Balzac remotely, but the fault of his style is that his work is rather more curious than beautiful and stronger than it is brilliant. These are projects of which I should not speak, as all my books are only the preparation for two, which I will finish if God lends me life. I mean this one and the Oriental story.

You must see the story of the journey that Enault has published on his return from Italy! He is a wag and a droll fellow, who will make an article in that cavalier fashion upon one with whom he has dined without first asking his permission. As for the article, it is simply stupid, and that one he wrote upon Bouilhet was no stronger. He underlines *bosom* and *rags,* exclaims "Eight children! O, Poesy!" paints the school where he thinks it probable there are a certain number of children that will be known to literature! No, if one does not keep himself from all this, *I say it in all seriousness*, there is danger of his becoming an idiot.

My father said repeatedly that he never would wish to be a doctor in a hospital for the insane, because if one dealt seriously with madness, he ended by becoming mad himself. It is the same in this case; from becoming too much disturbed by these imbeciles, there is danger of becoming such ourselves. Heavens! what a headache I have! I must go to bed! my thumb is hollowed by my pen and my neck is twisted.

I find Musset's observation of Hamlet that of a profound *bourgeois,* and this is the reason why: he reproaches the inconsistency of Hamlet, a sceptic, seeing with his eyes the soul of his father. But first, it was not the soul that he saw, but a phantom, a shadow, a thing, a materially living shadow, which has no connection either in popular or in poetic ideas with the abstract idea of the soul. It is we, metaphysicians and modern people, who speak this language; and then, Hamlet did not *question* at all the philosophic sense, he was *dreaming.* I believe this observation of Musset's is not his own but Malle-fille's; in the preface of his *Don Juan,* he is superficial, to my mind. A peasant in our day could see a phantom perfectly and, the next day in broad daylight, reflect in cold blood upon life and death, but not upon flesh and the soul. Hamlet was not reflecting upon the subtleties of some school, but upon human thoughts. On the contrary, it is this state of perpetual fluctuation in Hamlet, this vagueness in which he holds himself, this want of decision in will and solution in thought, which makes him sublime.

But *people of mind* will have their characters all of a piece and *consistent* (since they can have them so only in books). There is not an aim of the human soul which is not reflected in this conception. Ulysses is perhaps the strongest type in all ancient literature, and Hamlet of all modern.

If I were not so weary, I should express my thought at greater length; it is so easy to prattle about the beautiful; but to say in proper style "Shut the door," or "He has a desire to sleep," requires more genius than to make all the Courses of Literature in the world.

Criticism is the lowest round on the ladder of literature, nearly always in form and in moral value; incontestably it comes after the end-rhyme and the acrostic, which demand at least the work of some invention.

Now, adieu.

## TO LOUIS BOUILHET.

TROUVILLE, *Aug. 23*, 1853.

WHAT a confounded rain! How it falls! Everything is imbedded in water! From my window I can see bonnets passing shielded by red umbrellas; barques are putting out to sea; I hear the chains of the anchors which they are raising with general imprecations addressed to the bad weather. If it lasts three or four days more, which seems to me probable, we shall pack up and return home.

Admire here one of the polite ways of Providence which would be hard to believe: in whose house have I lodgings? In the house of a chemist! And of whom is he the pupil? Of Dupré! Like him, he deals in Seltzer water! "I am the only one in Trouville who manufactures Seltzer water," he says. In fact, at eight o'clock in the morning I am often awakened by the noise of corks which go off unexpectedly. Pif! paf! The kitchen is the laboratory as well as kitchen; a monstrous still stands humbly among the stewpans:

> The frightful length of its copper smoking,

and often they cannot put on the dinner-pot because of pharmaceutical preparations. In order to go into the yard, it is necessary to pass over baskets filled with bottles. There creaks a pump which wets your legs; two boys are rinsing decanters; a parrot repeats from morning till night: "Have you breakfasted, Jacko?" and finally, a brat about ten years old, the son of the house and the hope of the pharmacy, exercises in all sorts of athletics, such as raising himself from the ground by his teeth.

This journey to Trouville has brought the whole inner story of my life before me. I have dreamed much in this theatre of my passions. I now take leave of them forever, I hope; in the part of life that remains, there is time to say adieu to youthful sadness. I cannot conceal, however, that it has come back to me in waves, during the last three weeks. I have had two or three good afternoons in full sunlight, all alone upon the sand, where I found again some other sad things beside broken shells! But I have finished with it now, God be thanked! We shall now cultivate our garden and no more raise our head at the cry of the crows.

How I long to finish *Bovary, Anubis*, and my three prefaces, in order to enter a new period and give myself up to the "purely beautiful!" The idleness in which I have lived for some time gives me the cutting desire to transform through art all that is "myself," all that I have felt. I feel no need of writing my memoirs; my personality even repels me, and immediate objects seem hideous or stupid. I go back to former ideas. I arrange the barques into old-time ships. I undress the sailors who pass, to make savages of them walking naked upon the silver shores; I think of India, of China, of my Oriental story (of which fragments are coming to me), and I feel like undertaking gigantic epics.

But life is so short! I never can write as I wish, nor the quarter part of what I dream. All that force that we feel and that stifles us must die with us without being allowed to overflow!

I revisited yesterday a village two hours' journey from here, where I went with that good Orlowski when I was eleven years old. Nothing was changed about the houses, the cliff, or the fishing-boats. The women at the wash-house were sewing in the same position, the same number were beating their soiled linen in the same blue water, and it rained a little as in former times. It seemed, at certain moments that the universe had become immovable, that everything had become a statue, and that we alone were living. And how insolent nature is! What waggishness on her impudent visage! One tortures his mind trying to comprehend the abyss that separates him from her, but something comes up more farcical still, that is, the abyss that separates us from ourselves. When I think that here, in this place, on looking at this white wall off-setting the green, I had some heart throbs, and that I was full of "poesy," I am amazed, lost in a vertigo, as if I had suddenly discovered myself on the peak of a wall two thousand feet high.

This little work that I am doing, I shall complete this winter, when you are no longer there, poor old man! to arrange, burn, and, classify all my scribblings. With the *Bovary* finished, the age of reason will begin. And then, why encumber ourselves with so many souvenirs? The past eats up too much and we are never in the present, which alone is important in life. How I philosophise! I have need to, since you are there! It is difficult to write; words are wanting, and I should prefer being extended on my bear-skin, near you, discoursing "melancholically" together.

Do you know that in the last number of the *Review* our friend Leconte was very badly treated?

They are definitely low rascals; and "the phalanx" is a dog-kennel. All the animals there are much more stupid than ferocious. You who love the word "paltry," be assured that is what it is.

Write me an immeasurable letter as soon as you can, and embrace yourself for me; adieu.

## TO MADAME X.

CROISSET, *Wednesday evening, Midnight.*

I HAVE taken up the *Bovary* again, and since Monday have five pages almost done; *almost* is the word, for it is necessary to take it up again. How difficult it is! I fear that my *comices* (primary meetings) may be too long; it is a hard place. I have there all the personages of my book in action and in dialogue, mingled with one another, and beyond them all is a great landscape which envelopes them; if I can succeed with it, it will be very symphonic.

Bouilhet has finished the descriptive part of his *Fossils.* His mastodon ruminating in the moonlight on a prairie is enormously full of poesy and will be, perhaps, to the public, the most effective of all his pieces! There only remains the philosophic part, which is the last. About the middle of next month, he will go to Paris to select a lodging where he can install himself the first of November. Would that I were in his place!

Decidedly, the article by Verdun on Leconte (which I have an idea is Jourdan's) is more stupid than hostile; I have laughed much at the comparison they make with the *beautiful lines* of the *Fall of an Angel;* what bearish politeness! As for the *Indian Poems* and the piece about *Dies iræ,* not a word. There is a certain ingenuousness about them, but why call the *sperchius, sperkhios?* That seems to me a true *janoterie.* What has become of the good Leconte,— is he progressing with his Celtic poem?

I have been re-reading some of Boileau, or rather all of Boileau, and with my pencil on the margin. This seems to me truly strong; one does not tire of what is well written, for style is life! It is the blood of the thought! Boileau has a little river, straight, not deep, but admirably limpid and well within its banks; and that is the reason why the waters have not dried up; nothing is lost of what he wishes to say. But how much art he has used and with so little effort!

Within the next two or three years, I intend to re-read attentively all the French classics and to an- notate them; this is work that will serve me in *my prefaces* (my work of literary critic, you know); I wish to state there the insufficiency of schools as they are, and to declare plainly that we make no claim to being one of them, we outsiders, nor is it necessary to be one of them. On the contrary, we are in the line of transmission; that seems to me strictly exact; it reassures and encourages me. What I admire in Boileau is what I admire in Hugo; and where one has been good, the other is excellent. There is only one standard of beauty; it is the same everywhere, although under different aspects, and more or less coloured by the reflections that dominate it. Voltaire and Chateaubriand, for example, were medi- ocre for the same reasons, etc. I shall try to make it seen why the æsthetic critic is so much behind the historic and scientific critic; he has never had any base. The knowledge that is wanting is that of the anatomy of style; to know how a phrase is constructed, and where it should be attached. They study manikins and translations with professors,— imbeciles incapable of holding the instrument of the science they teach (I mean the pen), and the result is, they lack life!

Love! Love! the secret of the good God which does not easily give itself up,— the soul, without which nothing is understood.

When I have finished that (and the *Bovary* and *Anubis* first of all), I shall without doubt, enter into a new phase, and it seems slow getting there; I, who write so slowly, am gnawed by my plans. I wish to produce two or three long, epic antiques — romances in a grandiose setting, where the action may be forcefully fertile and the details rich in themselves, and luxurious and tragic as a whole; books of grand mural painting, of heroic size.

There was in the *Revue de France* (a fragment by Michelet upon Danton) a judgment of Robespierre that pleased me much; it stamped him as being in himself a government; and it was for that reason that all Republican governmental maniacs loved him. Mediocrity cherishes rules, but I hate them. I feel myself against them and against all restrictions, corporations, caste, hierarchy, levels, and droves, with an execration that fills my soul; it is on this side, perhaps, that I comprehend the martyr.

Adieu, beautiful ex-democrat.

## TO MADAME X.

CROISSET, *Wednesday, Midnight.*

HAVE you still your tooth? Take steps, then, immediately to have it removed. There is nothing in the world worse than physical pain; and it is worse than death for a man, as Montaigne says, "to put himself under the skin of a calf to escape it." Pain has this evil: it makes us feel life too much; it gives us, as it were, a proof of malediction to ourselves which weighs upon us; it humiliates us, and that is sad for beings that are sustained solely by their pride.

Certain natures suffer not so much, and people without nerves are happy; but of how many things are they not deprived? According as one rises in the scale of being, the nervous faculty increases, that is, the faculty for suffering. Are to suffer and to think the same thing, then? Is genius, after all, only a refinement of pain, that is to say, a meditation of the objective through the soul?

The sadness of Molière came wholly from the human stupidity which he felt contained in himself; he suffered from the Diaforus and Tartuffes which passed before the eyes of his brain. Do you not suppose that the soul of a Veronese imbibes colour like a piece of stuff plunged into the boiling vat of a dyer? All things appear to him as if magnifying glasses were before his eyes. Michael-Angelo said that marble trembled at his approach; what is sure is, that he himself trembled when he approached marble. Mountains, for this man, had souls; they were of a corresponding nature and there was a sympathy between them like that between analogous elements. And this should establish, I know not where or how, some kind of volcanic train that would make poor human implements explode.

I find myself nearly half through my *comices*. I have made fifteen pages this month, not finished them,— but whether they are good or bad, I know not. How difficult dialogue is when one especially wishes it to have character; to paint by dialogue, and keep it lively, precise, and distinguished while it remains commonplace is monstrous, and I know of no one who has done this in a book. It is necessary to write the dialogue in comedy, while the narrative takes the epic style.

This evening I began again that accursed page about the lamps which I have already written four times; it is enough to make one beat his head against a wall! I am trying to paint (in one page) the gradations of the enthusiasm of a multitude watching a good man as he places many lamps in succession upon the outside of the mayor's residence; it is necessary to make seen the crowd howling with astonishment and joy, and that without any apparent motive or reflection on the part of the author.

You are astonished at some of my letters, you say; you find in them well-written, pretty malice; well, I write what I think; but when it comes to writing for others, and making them speak as they would have spoken, what a difference! A moment ago, for example, I was trying to show in a dialogue a particular man who must be at the same time good-natured, commonplace, a little vulgar and pretentious! And beyond all this one must make sure that the point is clear. In a word, all the difficulties that we have in writing come from a lack of order. It is a conviction that I now have, that if you are troubled to give the right turn to an expression, it is sure that *you have not the idea*. A very clear image or sentiment in the head leads to the word on paper. The one flows from the other. "Whatever is well conceived," etc. . . . I have been re-reading this in old father Boileau; or rather I have read him entirely again (I am now on his prose works), and find him a master man and a great writer rather than a poet. But how stupid they have made him out! What paltry interpreters he has had! The race of college professors, pedants of pale ink, have lived upon him and stretched him thin, chattering over him like a cloud of locusts in a tree. He was not dense! No matter, he was solid of root and well planted, straight and well-poised.

The literary critic seems to me a thing to be made anew; those who have meddled with it are not of the trade, and while perhaps they know the anatomy of a phrase, they have not a drop of the physiology of style.

And about *La Servante?* Why was I afraid that it would not be long? Because it is better to be too long than too short, although the general defect of poets is the length, as it is of prose writers, which makes the first wearisome and the second disgusting. Lamartine, Eugene Suë. . . . Verse in itself is so convenient for disguising the absence of ideas! Analyse a beautiful passage of verse and another of prose, and you will see which is the fuller. Prose, art aside, must needs bristle with things to be discovered; but in verse the most trifling things appear. Thus we may say in comparison that the most unnoticed idea in a phrase of prose may suffice to make a whole sonnet; often, three or four plans are necessary in a prose work; do we expect to find this in poetry?'

I have at this moment a great rage for Juvenal. What style! what style! and what a language Latin is! I also flatter myself that I begin to understand Sophocles a little. As for Juvenal, it goes along smoothly enough, save here and there for some hidden meaning, which I quickly perceive. I should much like to know, and with many details, why Saulcy refused Leconte's article; what are the motives alleged? This must be interesting for us to know; try to get at the last word of the story.

Try to be better and to work better in Paris than in the country, for you have all your time to yourself. I grudge this poor Leconte his experience. In order to follow this trade as Bouilhet has for four years, eight and ten hours a day (and he had the boarding-house keepers at his back more than Leconte), I believe it is necessary to have the strongest constitution and a cerebral temperament of Titanic endurance. He will have merited glory as much as the other, but one can go to heaven only as a martyr, mounting on high with a crown of thorns, a pierced heart, bleeding hands and radiant face.

Adieu; a thousand kisses for thee!

## TO MADAME X.

CROISSET, *Wednesday, Midnight.*

MY HEAD is on fire, as I remember to have had it after passing long days on horseback, because to-day I have rudely ridden my pen. I have written since half-past twelve without stopping (save for five minutes at one time and another to smoke a pipe, and about an hour for dinner). My *comices* were such a trial to me that I have broken loose from them, even to the extent of calling them finished, both Greek and Latin; from to-day, I do no more of them; it is too hard! it would be the death of me, and I wish to go to see you.

Bouilhet pretends that it will be the most beautiful scene in the book. What I am sure of is that it will be new and that the intention is good. If ever the effects of a symphony were reported in a book, it will be here. It is necessary for the roar to be heard through it all: the bellowing of the bulls, the sighs of love, and the phrases of the administrators at once distinguishable; and over all the sunlight and the gusts of wind that fan the large bonnets into motion. The most difficult passages of *Saint Antony* were child's play in comparison. I have come to nothing dramatic except the interlacing of the dialogue and opposition in characters. I am now in the open; before another week, I shall have passed the knot upon which all depends. My brain seems too small to take in at a single glance this complex situation. I have written ten pages at a time, skipping from one phrase to another.

I am almost sure that Gautier did not see you in the street when he did not salute you; he is like myself, very near-sighted, and with me such things are customary. It would have been a gratuitous insolence, which is not his manner of behaviour; he is a great, good-natured man, very peaceful and very p——. As for espousing the animosities of a friend,

I strongly doubt it, from the way in which he spoke to me in the first place. The dedication, in spite of your opinion, proves nothing at all *pro* or *con*. The poor boy hangs to everything, tacks his name to everything that is descending this Nile! If anyone could strengthen me in my literary theories, it would be he. The farther off the time when Ducamp followed my advice, the more he goes down; for, between *Galaor* and the *Nil* there is a frightful decadence, and in the *Livre posthume*, which is between them, he is at his lowest, and the force of the young Delessert is no better. Jacotot's proposition was strangely revolting to me, and you were in the right. You try to be polite to a scamp like that? oh! no, no, no!

What a strange creature you are, dear friend, to send me diatribes still, as my chemist would call them. You ask me for a thing, I say "Yes," and you still continue to mutter! Oh, well! since you conceal nothing from me (which I approve), I will not conceal from you that this appears to me to be a bad habit with you. You wish to establish between relations of a different nature a bond of which I cannot see the sense or the utility. I do not at all comprehend how the kindnesses you show me when I am in Paris, affect my mother in any way. For three years I have been at the Schlesingers', where she has never set foot. In the same way, Bouilhet has been coming here every Sunday for eight years to sleep, dine and lunch, but we have not once seen his mother, who comes to Rouen nearly every month; and I assure you that my mother is not at all shocked. Nevertheless, it shall be according to your wish. I promise you, I swear it, that I will explain to her your reasons and that I will pray her to bring it about that you may see each other. As for the out-come, with the best will in the world, I can do nothing; perhaps you will please each other much, perhaps you will displease each other enormously. The good woman is not very approachable, and she has ceased to see not only all her old acquaintances but even her friends; I know only one of them and she does not live in the country.

I have just finished Boileau's Correspondence; he was less narrow among his intimates than in *Apollon*. I found there many confidences that corrected his judgments. *Télémaque* was harshly enough judged, etc., and he avows that Malherbe was not a poet. But have you not noticed of how little value is the correspondence of the great men of that time? It is, in fact, all commonplace. Lyricism in France is a new faculty; I believe that the education of the Jesuits has been a considerable misfortune to letters. They have taken nature away from art. Since the end of the sixteenth century, even to the time of Hugo, all books, however beautiful they may be, smell of the dust of the college. I am now going to re-read all my French and to take a long time to prepare my history of the poetical sentiment of France. It is necessary to write criticism as one would write a natural history, *with the absence of moral idea;* it is not for us to declaim upon such and such a form, but to show in what it consists, how it is attached to another and by what it lives (æstheticism awaits its Saint-Hilaire, that great man who has shown the legitimacy of monsters). When the human soul is treated with the impartiality with which physical science is treated in the study of material things, an immense step will have been taken; it is the only means by which humanity can put itself above itself. It will then consider itself frankly through the mirror of its works; it will be like God and judge from on high.

Well, I believe that feasible; perhaps, as in mathematics, we have only to find the method. Before all, it will be applicable to art and to religion, which are the two great manifestations of the idea. Suppose one begins thus: the first idea of God being given (the most simple possible), the first poetic sentiment being born (the most slender that could be), each finds at first its manifestation, and easily finds it in the savage infant, etc.; here is, then, the first point: you have already established relations. Now, if one were to continue, making count of all relative contingents, climate, language, etc.; then, from degree to degree one could come up to the art of the future, and the hypothesis of the Beautiful, to a clear conception of its reality, to that ideal type where all our effort should tend; but it is not for me to charge myself with this task, for I have other pens to cut.

Adieu.


## TO MADAME X.

CROISSET, *Friday, Midnight,* 1854.

I HAVE passed a sad week, not because of my work, but on your account, and because of my thoughts concerning you. I will tell you more privately the personal reflections that were the result of this state of mind.

You believe that I do not love you, my poor dear friend, and say that you are only a secondary consideration in my life. I have hardly any human affection for anyone greater than I feel for you, and as for affection towards woman, I swear to you that you stand first in my heart,—the only one; and I will affirm further: I never have felt a similar love — so prolonged, so sweet, above all, so profound.

As to the question of my immediate installation in Paris, I must give up the plan at once; it is *impossible* to carry it out now, to say nothing of the money I should have but have not. I know myself well: it would mean the loss of the winter; and perhaps of my book. Bouilhet spoke very easily about it, he, who is fortunate enough to be able to write anywhere, who for twelve years worked in continual confusion. But for me it is like beginning a new life. I am like a pan of milk — in order that cream shall rise, I must not be disturbed! But I say to you again: if you *wish* that I should come, now, instantly, for a month, two months, four months, cost what it may, I will go. If not, this is my plan: from the present time until I finish *Bovary,* I will visit you oftener,— eight times in two months, without missing a week, except for that time when you will not be able to see me until the end of January. Then we shall meet regularly through April, June, and September, and in a year I shall be very near the end of my book.

I have talked over all this with my mother. Do not accuse her, even in your heart, because she is on your side. I have concluded pecuniary settlements with her, and she is about to make arrangements for the care of my rooms, my linen, etc., for a year. I have engaged a servant whom I shall take to Paris, so you see that my resolution is not wholly unshakeable, and if I am not buried here under about three hundred pages, you may see me before long installed in the capital. I shall disturb nothing at my rooms, because I always work best there, and I shall probably pass most of my time there, on account of my mother, who is growing old; so reassure yourself, I shall show enough filial affection, and be very good!

Do you know whither the sadness of all this has led me, and what I should like to do? I should like to throw literature to the winds forever, to do nothing more, but go and live with you! I say to myself; Is art worth so much trouble, so much weariness for me, so many tears for her? Of what use is all this effort, perhaps to arrive only at mediocrity in the end? For I own to you that I am not cheerful; I have sad doubts at times regarding myself and my work. I have just re-read *Novembre*, from curiosity. I did the same thing eleven years ago to-day. I had so far forgotten it that it seemed quite new to me, but it is not good, and the effect is not satisfactory. I see no way of re-writing it; I should be compelled to recast it entirely, because although here and there I find a good phrase, a good comparison, there is no homogeneity of style. Conclusion: *Novembre* will go the same way with *Sentimental Education,* and will remain with it indefinitely in my portfolio. Ah, what good sense I showed in my youth not to publish! How I should have blushed for it now!

I am about to write a monumental letter to the "Crocodile." Hasten to send me yours, because it is several days since my mother wrote to Madame Farmer, and she persecutes me to let her read my letter before I send it away.

I am re-reading Montaigne. It is singular how I am filled with the spirit of this good fellow! Is this a coincidence, or is it because when I was eighteen years old I read only Montaigne during a whole twelvemonth? I am really astonished, however, to find very often in his writings the most delicate analysis of my own sentiments. He has the same tastes, the same opinions, the same manner of living, the same manias. There are persons I admire more than Montaigne, but there is no one I would evoke more gladly, or with whom I could talk better.

Thine ever.

## TO LAURENT PICHAT
(Director of the *Revue de Paris*.)

CROISSET, *Thursday evening*, 1856.

MY DEAR FRIEND: I have just received the *Bovary*, and I feel that I must thank you immediately (for if I am somewhat churlish, I am not an ingrate). You have rendered me a great service in accepting this work, such as it is, and I shall not forget it.

Confess that you have found me, and that you still find me (more than ever, perhaps) possessed of a ridiculous amount ot vehemence. I should like to own some day that you are right; I promise that when that time comes I will make you the most abject excuses! But understand, dear friend, that it was only an experiment I attempted, and I hope the workmanship is not too crude.

Will you believe me when I tell you that the ignoble realism you find in my story, the reproduction of which disgusts you, revolts me quite as much? If you knew me better, you would know that I hold commonplace existence in execration. I always seclude myself from it as much as possible. But, for æsthetic purposes, I wished this time — and only this time — to exploit it from its very foundation. So I have undertaken the matter in a heroic way; I listened to the minutest details; I accepted all, said all, painted all, — an ambitious attempt.

I explain myself badly, but it is enough that you comprehend the reason for my resistance of your criticisms, judicious as they were. You will make another book for me! You struck at the poetic foundation whence springs the type (as a philosopher would say) from which the work was conceived. In short, I should have failed in what I owe to myself, and also in what I owe to you, if I had yielded as an act of deference and not of conviction.

Art demands neither complaisance nor politeness, — nothing but faith — faith and liberty! And on that point we may join hands!

Under an unfruitful tree, whose branches are always green, I am          Faithfully yours.

## TO ERNEST FEYDEAU.

1857.

MY GOOD FRIEND: I believe it is always considered proper to wash one's soiled linen. Now I will wash mine immediately. You say you have been "very much vexed" at me, and you must feel so still, if you really suppose that I had, in company with Aubeyet, said anything against either yourself or your works. I am writing this in all seriousness. Such an accusation chokes me, wounds me. I am made so —I cannot help it. Know, then, that such cowardly conduct is completely antipathetic to me. I do not allow anyone to say, in my presence, anything about my friends that I would not say myself to their faces. And if a stranger opens his mouth to lie about them, I close it for him immediately. The contrary custom is the usual thing, I know, but it is not my way. Let us have no more discussion of this! If you do not know me better than that by this time, all the worse for you! Let us consider less serious matters, and give me your word of honour, for the future, never again to judge me as if I were a stranger.

Know also, O Feydeau! that I am not a bit of a *farceur*. There is no animal in the world more serious than I! Sometimes I laugh, but I joke very little, and less now than ever before. I am sick, as a result of fear; all sorts of anguish fill my being. I am about to write once more!

No, my good fellow, I'm not so stupid! I shall not show you anything of my story of Carthage until the last line is written, because I am already assailed with doubts enough about it without adding to them those you would express. Your observations would make me "lose the ball." As to the archæology, that will be "probable." And that's all! Provided no one can prove that I have written absurdities, that is all I ask. As to the botanical queries that may arise, I can laugh at them. I have seen with my own eyes all the plants and all the trees that I need for my purpose.

Besides, all this matters very little; it is quite a secondary consideration. A book may be full of enormities and blunders, and yet be none the less beautiful. If this doctrine were admitted, it would be considered deplorable, of course; especially in France, where reigns the pedantry of ignorance! But I see in the contrary tendency (which is mine, alas!) a great danger. The study of the external makes us forget the soul. I would give the half-ream of notes that I have written during the past five months, and the ninety-eight books that I have read, to be, for three seconds only, really stirred by the passion and emotion experienced by my heroes! Let us guard against the temptation to deal with trifles, or we shall find ourselves belonging to the coffee-cup school of the Abbé Delille. There is at present a school of painting which, in order to make us admire Pompeii, adopts a style more *rococo* than that of Girodet. I believe, then, that one must love nothing, that is, we should preserve the strictest impartiality towards all objectives.

Why do you persist in irritating my nerves by saying that a field of cabbages is more beautiful than a desert? Permit me first to beg that you will go and look at the desert before talking about it! And even if there is anything as beautiful, go there just the same. But in your expression of a preference for the *bourgeois* vegetable, I see only an attempt to enrage me, which has been quite successful.

You will not have from me any criticism written on *l'Été* because, first, it would take too much of my time; and second, I might say things that would vex you. Yes, I am afraid of compromising myself, for I am not sure of anything, and that which displeased me might, after all, be the best thing I could have said. I shall wait for your brutal and unwavering opinion regarding *l'Automne*. *Le Printemps* pleased and entranced me, without any restrictions. As to *l'Été*, I have made a few.

Now,— but I must stop, because my observations may be directed against an affair that is already settled, which perhaps is a good thing — I do not know. And as there is nothing in the world more tiresome or stupid than an unjust criticism, I will withhold mine, although it might have been good. So that is all, my dear old boy! You accused me in your mind of a cowardly action. This time you have reason to call me cowardly, but the cowardice is only that of prudence.

Are you amusing yourself? Do you employ your preservatives, impure man? What a wicked fellow is my friend Feydeau, and how I envy him! As for me, I worry myself immeasurably. I feel old, tired, withered. I am as sombre as a tomb and as crabbed as a hedgehog.

I have just read Cohan's book from one end to the other. I know that it is very faithful, very good, very wise, but I prefer the old *Vulgate,* because of the Latin. How swelling it is, compared with this poor, puny, pulmonic little Frenchman! I will show you two or three mistranslations (or rather, embellishments) in the said *Vulgate,* which have more beauty than the real meaning.

Go on and amuse yourself, and pray to Apollo to inspire me, for I am sadly flattened out.

Thine ever.

## TO ERNEST FEYDEAU.

CROISSET, *Sunday evening,* 1858.

WHAT has become of you? As for myself, I have passed nearly four days in sleeping, because of extreme fatigue; then I wrote my notes of travel, and my lord Bouilhet has come to visit me.

During the week that he has been here we have been digging ferociously. I must tell you that the story of Carthage is to be completely changed, or rather, to be written over again, as I have destroyed the whole of the original! It was absurd, impossible, false!

I believe now that I have struck the right note at last. I begin to comprehend my personages, and already feel a great interest in them. I do not know when I shall finish this colossal work. Perhaps not before two or three years. From now on, I shall beg everyone that meets me not to talk to me. I should like to send out notes announcing my death!

My course of action is planned. For me, the public, outside impressions, and time, exist no more. To work!

I have re-read *Fanny,* at a single sitting, although I already knew it by heart. My impression has not changed, but the whole effect seems to be more rapid in movement, which is good. Do not disturb yourself about anything, nor think any more about this. When you come here next, I shall allow myself to point out to you two or three insignificant details.

About the middle of next week, *Montarcy* is to be played. Then, at the beginning of next month,

Bouilhet will return to Mantes, and my mother will go to Trouville for a little visit of about a week. After that, my dear sir, we shall expect you.

Will that be convenient and agreeable? Why have you not sent me any news of yourself, you rascal? What are you writing? What are you doing? How about Houssaye? etc.

As for myself, I take a river bath every day. I swim like a triton. My health never has been better. My spirits are good, and I am full of hope. When one is in good health he should store up a reserve of courage, in order to meet disappointments in the future. They will come, alas!

I believe that in the Rue Richer there is a photographer who sells views of Algiers. If you could find me a view of Medragen (the tomb of the Numidian kings), near Algiers, and send it to me, I should be very grateful.

## TO JULES DUPLAN.

1858.

I HAVE arrived, in my first chapter, at the description of my little woman. I am polishing up her costume — a task that pleases me. It has set me up not a little. I spread myself out, like a pig, on the stones by which I am surrounded; I think that the words "purple" or "diamond" are in every phrase in the chapter. And gold lace! — but I must not say any more about it.

I shall certainly have finished my first chapter by the time you see me again (that will not be before

December), and perhaps I shall have advanced con-
siderably with the second, although it will be impossible to write it in haste. This book [*Salammbô*] is
above all things a grouping of effects. My processes
in beginning this romance are not good, but it is necessary to make the surroundings *seem real* at the very
outset. After that there will be enough of details and
ornament to give the thing a natural and simple effect.

Young Bouilhet has begun his fourth act.

Have you had a good laugh at the fast ordered by
Her Majesty Queen Victoria?

I think it is one of the most magisterial pieces of
absurdity that I ever have known; it is amazing!
O Rabelais, where is thy vast mouth?

### TO MADEMOISELLE LEROYER DE CHANTEPIE.

*December 26, 1858.*

You may think that I have forgotten you, but I
have done nothing of the kind! My thoughts are often
turned towards you, and I address myself to the "un-
known God," of whom St. Paul speaks, in prayers
for the comfort and satisfaction of your spirit. You
hold in my heart a very high and pure place; you
would hardly believe me if I should tell you what a
marvellous depth of sentiment your first letters touched
in me. I must tell you of all that I feel, at some
better time than this. We must meet soon, to clasp
each other's hands, that I may press a kiss upon your
brow!

This is what has happened since I wrote my last letter:

I was in Paris for ten days, where I assisted and co-operated in the last performances of *Hélène Peyron*. This is a very beautiful play, and it is also a great success. Making calls, reading the journals, etc., kept me very busy, and I returned here worn out, as usual, and as to the moral effect, I was disgusted with all that uproar. I fell upon my *Salammbô* again with fury.

My mother has gone to Paris, and for a month I have been entirely alone. I have begun my third chapter, and the story is to have twelve. You can judge how much remains for me to do. I have thrown the preface into the fire, although I worked two months on it this summer. But I am just beginning, *at last,* to feel entertained by my own work. Every day I rise at noon, and I retire at four o'clock in the morning. A white bear is not more solitary and a god is not more calm. It was time! I think of nothing but Carthage, and it is necessary that I should. To write a book has always meant to me the necessity of imagining myself to be actually living in the place described. This will explain my hesitations, my distress of mind, and my slowness.

I shall not return to Paris until the last of February. Between now and that time you will see in the *Revue Contemporaine* a romance by my friend Feydeau, which is dedicated to me, and which I hope you will read.

Do you keep yourself informed as to the works of Renan? They would interest you, and so would the new book by Flourens, on the *Siège de l'âme.*

Can you guess what occupies me at present? The maladies of serpents (always for my Carthage book)! I am about to write to Tunis to-day on this subject. When one wishes to be absolutely accurate in such writing, it costs something! All this may seem rather puerile, or even foolish. But what is the use of living if one may not indulge in dreams?

Adieu! A thousand embraces. Write to me as often as you wish, and as freely as you can.

## TO ERNEST FEYDEAU.

CROISSET, *Thursday*.

I HAVE not forgotten you at all, my dear old boy, but I am working like thirty niggers! I have finally finished my interminable fourth chapter from which I have stricken out that which I liked best. Then, I have made the plan of the fifth, written a quantity of notes, etc. The summer has not begun badly. I believe that the work will go smoothly now, but perhaps I delude myself. What a book! Heavens! It is difficult!

Yes, I find, contrary to D'Aurevilly, that there is now a question of hypocrisy and nothing else. I am alarmed, amazed, scandalised at the transcendent poltroonery that possesses the human race. Everyone fears "being compromised." This is something new, —at least, to such a degree as appears. The desire for success, the necessity, even, of succeeding, *because of the profit to be made,* has so greatly demoralised literature that one becomes stupid through timidity. The idea of failure or of incurring censure makes the timid writer shake in his shoes. "That's· all very well for you to say, you, who collect your rents," I think I hear you remark. A very clever response, the inference of which is that morality is to be relegated to a place among objects of luxury! The time is no more when writers were dragged to the Bastille. It might be rebuilt, but no one could be found to put in it.

All this will not be lost. The deeper I plunge into antiquity, the more I feel the necessity of reforming modern times, and I am ready to roast a number of worthy citizens!

Do not think any more about *Daniel*. It is finished. It will be read, be sure of that.

When you come to Croisset, before setting out for Luchon (about the beginning of July, I suppose), bring me the detailed plan of *Catherine*. I have several ideas on your style in general and on your future book in particular.

You are a rascal! You compromise my name in public places! I shall attack you in a court of justice for a theft of titles.

I have two pretty neighbours who have read *Daniel*, twice running. And the coachmen of Rouen fall off their seats while reading *Fanny* (historic)!

*À propos* of morality, have you read that the inhabitants of Glasgow have petitioned Parliament to suppress the models of nude women in the schools of drawing?

Adieu, old boy; dig hard!

What news of your wife? Why is she at Versailles? It is an atrocious place, colder than Siberia.

## TO EDMOND AND JULES DE GONCOURT.

CROISSET, *May*, 1860.

I MUST tell you of the pleasure I had in reading your two books. I found them charming, full of new details and having an excellent style, showing at the same time nervous power and lofty imagination. That is history, it seems to me, and original history.

One sees in them always the soul within the body; the abundance of details does not stifle the psychological side. The moral is revealed beneath the facts, without declamation or digression. It *lives,*— a rare merit.

The portrait of Louis XV., that of Bachelier, and above all, that of Richelieu, seem to me to be products of the most finished art.

How much you make me love Madame de Mailly! She actually excites me! "She was one of those beauties . . . like the divinities of a bacchante!" Heavens! You certainly write like angels!

I know of nothing in the world that has interested me more than the finale of *Madame de Châteauroux.*

Your judgment of the Pompadour will rest without appeal, I fancy. What could anyone say after you?

That poor Du Barry! How you love her, do you not? I love her, too, I must confess. How fortunate you are, to be able to occupy yourselves with all that sort of thing, instead of diving into nothingness, or working upon nothingness, as I must work.

It is altogether charming of you to send me the book, to have so much talent, and to love me a little! I clasp your four hands as warmly as possible, and am ever your

G. FLAUBERT,

Friend of Franklin and of Marat; factionist, and anarchist *of the first order*, and for twenty years a disorganiser of despotism on two hemispheres!!!


TO EDMOND AND JULES DE GONCOURT.

CROISSET, *July 3,* 1860.

SINCE you appear to be interested in my *Carthage,* this is what I have to tell you about it:

I believe that my eyes have been larger than my belly! To present the *reality* is almost impossible with such a subject. One's only resource is to make the thing poetic, but there is danger of falling into the way of employing the old, well-known tricks of speech that have been used from *Télémaque* to the *Martyrs.*

I say nothing of the archælogical researches, the labour of gathering which must not be evident, nor of the language and the form, which are almost impossible to handle. If I tried to write with absolute accuracy of detail, the work would be obscure; I should be compelled to use abstruse terms, and to stuff the volumes with notes. And if I should preserve the usual French literary tone, the work would become simply banal. Problem! as Father Hugo would say·

In spite of all that, I continue, but I am devoured by anxiety and doubts. I console myself with the thought that at least I have attempted to do something worth while. That is all.

The standard of the Doctrine will be boldly carried this time, I assure you! But it proves nothing, it says nothing, it is neither historic, nor satirical, nor humorous. On the other hand, is it not stupid?

I have just begun Chapter VIII., after which seven still remain to be written. I shall not finish the work before eighteen months have passed.

It was not a mere bit of politeness on my part when I congratulated you on your work. I love history madly! The dead are far more agreeable to me than the living. Whence comes this seduction of the past? Why have you made me fall in love with the mistresses of Louis XV.? A love like this is, now I think of it, a decided novelty in human emotion. The historic sense dates from yesterday, and it is perhaps the best characteristic of the nineteenth century.

What are you doing now? As for myself, I am deep in Kabbala, in Mischna, in the military tactics of the ancients, etc. (a mass of reading that is of no particular use to me, but which I undertook through the urgency of my conscience, and also a little to amuse myself). I worry myself over the assonances that I find in my prose; my life is as flat as the table upon which I write. The days follow one another, each one appearing to be exactly like the preceding, externally, at least. In my despair, I sometimes dream of travel. Sad remedy!

Both of you seem to me to have the air of stultifying yourselves virtuously in the bosom of your family, among the delights of the country! I comprehend that sort of thing, having undergone it several times.

Shall you be in Paris from the first of August to the 25th?

While waiting for the joy of seeing you, I clasp your hands with true affection.

## TO ERNEST FEYDEAU.

CROISSET, *Sunday, July* 20, 1860.

I REPLY immediately to your pretty letter, received this morning, to congratulate you, my dear sir, on the life you lead! Accept the homage of my envy.

Since you ask me about *Salammbô,* this is how it stands. I have just finished the ninth chapter, and am preparing the material for the tenth and eleventh, which I intend to write this winter, living here all alone, like a bear.

I am occupied now with a quantity of reading, which I get through with great rapidity. For the last three days I have done nothing but swallow Latin, following, at the same time, my studies of the early Christians. As to the Carthaginians, I really believe I have exhausted all texts on the subject. After my romance is finished, it would be easy for me to write a large volume of criticisms of these books, with strong citations. For instance, no longer ago than to-day, a passage in Cicero led me to discover a form of Tanith of which I had had no previous knowledge.

I become wise—and sad! Yes, I now lead a holy existence—I, who was born with so many appetites! But sacred literature has become a part of my very being.

I pass my time in putting stones on the pit of my stomach, to prevent the feeling of hunger! This makes me fairly stupid at times.

As to my "copy" (since that is the term), frankly, I do not know what to think. I fear I may fall into the way of making continual repetitions, of eternally rehashing the same things. Sometimes my phrases seem to be all cut after the same fashion, and likely to bore anyone to death. My will does not weaken, but I find it very difficult to please myself. I feel like *eating* my own words.

You may judge of my agitation just now, when I tell you that I am actually preparing a grand *coup*, the finest effect in the book. It must be at once brutal and chaste, mystical yet realistic,—a kind of effect that never has been produced before, yet absolutely real and convincing.

That which I predicted has come true; you are enamoured of Arabian manners and morals! How much time you will lose, after you return, dreaming, beside the fire, of dark eyes beneath a cloudless sky!

Send me a line as soon as you return to Paris. You said you expected to arrive by the end of the month. That time is now here. We must not let any longer time elapse without seeing each other. Bouilhet's play will have its first performance about the 15th or the 20th of November.

My mother and my niece are well, and thank you for your kind remembrance. As to my niece, I believe I shall be made a great-uncle next April. I am becoming a veteran, a sheikh, an old man, an idiot!

May you enjoy the last days of your journey and have a good voyage home. I embrace thee!


## TO MADEMOISELLE LEROYER DE CHANTEPIE.

CROISSET, *September* 8, 1860.

I RECEIVED on Tuesday morning your letter of the first of September. It saddened me to read the expression of your grief. Besides your private sorrow, you are surrounded by exterior annoyances, as I understand, since you are forced to perceive the ingratitude and selfishness of those who are under obligations to you. I must tell you that such is *always* the case, — a very poor consolation, it is true! But the conviction that rain is wet and that a rattlesnake is dangerous has its share in helping us to support our miseries. Why is this so? But here we attempt to encroach upon the omniscience of God!

Let us try to forget evil, and turn to the sunshine and the good we may find in life. If a malicious person wounds you, try to remember the kindness of some noble heart, and fill your mind with that recollection.

You tell me that you find absolutely no sympathy of ideas. That is one reason why you should live in Paris. One always finds there some person to whom one can talk. You were not made for

provincial life. I am convinced that among other surroundings you would have suffered less. Each soul
has its own atmosphere. You must suffer keenly, in
the midst of the folly, lies, calumnies, jealousies, and
indescribable pettiness which are almost the inevitable
accompaniment of *bourgeois* life in small towns. Of
course, that sort of thing exists in Paris also, but in
another form—less direct and less irritating.

There is still time to form a good resolution. Do
not continue to live "on foot" as you have lived
heretofore. Tear yourself away! Travel! Do you
think you may die on the way? Ah, well, never
mind! No, no, believe me when I tell you that you
would be better for it, physically and morally. But
you need a master, who would order you to go, and
force you to it! I know you as well as if I had lived
with you twenty years. Is this presumption on my
part,—an excessive sympathy that I feel for you?

I assure you that I am very fond of you, and that
I wish you to know, if not happiness, at least tranquillity. But it is not possible to enjoy the least
serenity with your habit of delving incessantly among
the greatest mysteries. You kill both your body and
your soul in trying to conciliate two contradictory
things: religion and philosophy. The liberalism of
your mind revolts against the old rubbish of dogma,
and your natural mysticism takes alarm at the extreme consequences whither your reason leads you.
Try to confine yourself to science, to pure science;
learn to love facts for themselves. Study ideas as
naturalists study insects. Such contemplation may be
full of tenderness. The breasts of the Muses are full
of milk; and that liquid is the beverage of the strong.
And—once more—leave the place where your soul

is stifling. Go at once, instantly, as if the house were afire!
. Think of me sometimes, and believe always in my sincere affection.


TO EDMOND AND JULES DE GONCOURT.

1861.

You must have found a letter from me at your house in Paris, as I wrote to you the same day I received your book (last Monday), after reading it from one end to the other without hastening.

I was enchanted with it! It has an upspringing power that never flags for an instant. As to the analysis, it is perfect—it fairly dazzles me. In my former letter you will find my impression given immediately after the first reading. I should now be reading it a second time, if my mother had not three ladies under her roof, who are regaling themselves with it! It will certainly appeal to the fair sex, and therefore will be a success—I believe that is the general idea. But I have found opportunities to dip into your *Philomène* here and there, and I know the book perfectly. My opinion is this: You have done that which you wished to do, and have done it with great success.

Do not have any anxiety about it. Your *réligieuse* is not banal, thanks to the explanation at the beginning. That was the danger, but you have avoided it.

But that which lends the book its simplicity has perhaps restricted its breadth a little. Beside Sister

Philoméne I should have wished to see contrasted the generality of *réligieuses,* who scarcely resemble her. And that is the only objection I have to make. It is true that you have not entitled your book: *Morals of a Hospital!* This may be the cause of some criticism.

I cannot find words to tell you how pleased I am with your work. I notice a new effect of realism in it,—the power to describe the natural connection of facts. Your method of doing this is excellent. Perhaps the strongest interest of the work springs from this.

What an imbecile was Levy! But he is very amusing, all the same.

No, there are not too many "horrors" (for my personal taste, there are not even enough!—but that is a question of temperament). You stopped just at the very limit. There are exquisite traits,—the old man who coughs, for instance, and the head surgeon among his pupils, etc. The conclusion is superb—I mean the death of Barnier.

It was necessary, perhaps, for you to make your romance in six volumes, but it must have been a wearisome piece of work. They say it is impossible to please everyone; but I am convinced that your *Sister Philoméne* will have a great success, and shall not be at all surprised at it.

I have said nothing about your style, for it has been a long time since I first congratulated you upon that!

Romaine excites my admiration beyond bounds. "Ah! To touch, as you touched, to cut, as you cut there yourself." Here a true and deep note is sounded.

I am as proud of you as I am displeased with myself. Alas! My good friends, things do not go well.

It seems to me that *Salammbô* is stupid enough to kill one! There is too much talk of the unsettled conditions of ancient times, always battles, always furious people. One longs for cradling verdure and a milk diet! Berquin would seem delicious after this. In short, I am not contented. I believe my plan is bad, but it is too late to change it, because everything now is fully settled.

What do you intend to do next? How goes *La Jeune Bourgeoise?* Write to me when you have nothing better to do, for I think of you very often.

Adieu! A thousand thanks, and a thousand sincere compliments! I embrace you.

## TO ERNEST FEYDEAU.

1861.

WHAT a man was old Father Hugo! Heavens! what a poet! I have just devoured his two volumes. I need you! I need Bouilhet! I need some intelligent auditor! I want to bawl three thousand verses as no one else ever has bawled them! Did I say bawl?—I meant *howl!* I do not recognize myself— I do not know what possesses me! Ah! that has done me good!

I have found three superb details which are not at all historic and which are in my *Salammbô*. I must cut them out, else some one would be sure to accuse me of plagiarism. It is the poor that are always charged with stealing!

My work is progressing rather better. I am now engrossed in a battle of elephants, and I assure you that I kill men off like flies! I pour blood in torrents!

I wished to write you a long letter, my poor old boy, about the annoyances you suffer, which seem to me rather serious, but frankly, it is time I went to bed. It will soon be four o'clock in the morning. Father Hugo has turned my brain topsy-turvy!

I, too, have had for some time annoyances and anxieties that are not slight. But — *Allah Kherim!*

You appear to me to be in good condition. You are right. As your book will not be about Belgium (the scene, I mean), it will have a freer colour and unity. But think seriously after that of your proposed work on the Bourse, of which there is a crying need.

## TO MADAME ROGER DES GENETTES.

1861.

A GOOD subject for a romance is one that is embodied in one idea, springing up like a single jet of water. It is the "mother idea," whence come all that follow. One is by no means free to write of such or such a thing; he does not *choose* his subject. This is something that the public and the critics do not comprehend, but the secret of all masterpieces lies in the concordance between the subject and the temperament of the author.

You are right; we must speak with respect of *Lucrece;* I can compare it only to Byron, and Byron had not his gravity, nor his sincerity, nor his sadness. The melancholy of the olden time seems to me more profound than that of our day, which implies, more or less, the idea of immortality beyond the grave. But to the ancients the grave was infinity; their dreams were conceived and enacted against a black and unchangeable background. No cries, no convulsions, nothing but the fixity of a thoughtful visage! The gods no longer existed, and the Christ had not yet come; and the ancients, from Cicero to Marcus Aurelius, lived at a unique epoch when man alone was all-powerful. I do not find anything like such grandeur as this; but that which renders *Lucrece* intolerable is its philosophy, which the author presents as positive. It is because he does not suspect that it is weak; he wishes to explain, to conclude! If he had resembled Epicurus only in mind and not in system, all parts of his work would have been immortal and radical. No matter! Our modern poets are weak and puny compared with such a man!


TO MADAME ROGER DES GENETTES.

CROISSET, 1862.

To YOU I can say everything! Well, our god has come down a peg! *Les Misérables* exasperates me, yet one cannot say a word against it, for fear of being thought a *mouchard!* The position of the author is impregnable, unassailable. I, who have passed my life in adoring him, am actually indignant at him at present, and must burst out somehow!

I find in this book neither verity nor grandeur. As to style, it seems to me intentionally incorrect and

low, as if the story had been written thus to flatter
the popular taste. Hugo has a good word and kindly
attention for everyone: Saint Simonians, Philippists,
even for innkeepers,—all receive equal adulation, and
the types are like those found only in tragedies.
Where are there any prostitutes like Fantine, convicts
like Valjean, and politicians like the stupid donkeys
of the A, B, C? Nowhere do we find the real suffering of the *soul*. These are only manikins, sugar
dolls, beginning with Monseigneur Bienvenu. In a
rage of socialism, Hugo calumniates the Church as he
calumniates misery.

Where is the bishop who asks a benediction from
a convention? Where is the factory that turns away
a girl because she has a child? And the digressions!
How many of these do we find! The passage about
manure should interest Pelletan!

This book was written for the low socialist class
and for the philosophical-evangelical vermin. What a
pretty character is Monsieur Marius, living for three
days on a cutlet, and Monsieur Enjolras, who never
had given but two kisses in his life, poor fellow!

As to the conversations, they are good, but they
are all alike. The eternal repetitions of Père Gille-
normant, the final delirium of Valjean, the humour of
Cholomiès and of Gantaise—it is all in the same
strain. Always a straining after effects, attempts at
jokes, an effort at gaiety, but nothing really comic.
There are lengthy explanations of things quite outside
the subject, and a lack of details that should be in-
dispensable. Then there are long sermons, saying
that universal suffrage would be a very fine thing, and
that it is necessary to instruct the masses,—all of
which is repeated to satiety.

Decidedly, this book, in spite of some beautiful passages, is childish. Personal observation is a secondary quality in literature, but one should not allow himself to paint society so falsely when he is the contemporary of Balzac and of Dickens. It was a splendid subject, but what calm philosophy it demanded in its treatment, and what breadth of scientific vision! It is true that Father Hugo disdains science,—and he proves it!

In my mind this confirms Descartes or Spinoza.

Posterity will not pardon him for attempting to be a thinker, in spite of his nature. Where has the rage for philosophic prose conducted him? And what kind of philosophy? That of Prudhomme, of the Bonhomme Richard, or of Béranger. He is no more of a thinker than Racine, or La Fontaine, whom he considers mediocre; that is, in this book he flows with the current, even as they; he gathers all the banal ideas of his epoch, and with such persistence that he forgets his work and his art.

This is my opinion; I keep it to myself, you understand. Anyone that handles a pen must feel too much gratitude towards Hugo to permit himself to criticise him; but I find that externally, at least, even the gods grow old!

I await your reply—and your anger!

## TO THEOPHILE GAUTIER.

1863.

WHAT a charming article, my dear Théo, and how can I thank you for it? If anyone had said to me, when I was twenty years old, that Théophile Gautier, with whom my imagination was filled, would write such things about me, I should have become delirious with pride!

Have you read the third philippic of Sainte-Beuve? But your panegyric of Trajan avenges me.

May I expect you the day after to-morrow? Tell Toto to give me an answer regarding this.

Your old friend.

## TO THÉOPHILE GAUTIER.

*Monday evening,* 1863.

MY OLD THÉO: Do not come Wednesday. I am invited to dine with the Princess Mathilde that evening, and we should not have time for a chat before dinner. Let us put it off until Saturday. Ducamp has been notified.

My reply to my lord Frœhner will appear in *l'Opinion* next Saturday, or perhaps Thursday. I believe that you will not be displeased with the phrase that alludes to you.

Is it understood, then — Saturday?

## TO THÉOPHILE GAUTIER.

CROISSET, *April 3,* 1864.

How goes it, dear old master? How comes on the *Fracasse?* What do you think of *Salammbô?* Is there anything new to say about that young person? The *Figaro-Programme* has mentioned it again, and Verdi is in Paris.

As soon as you have finished your romance, come to my cabin and stay a week (or more) according to your promise, and we will lay out the scenario. I shall expect you in May. Let me know two days in advance before you come.

I am dreaming of writing two books, without having done any actual work upon them. I have nails in my throat — if I may so express myself.

It seems to me a very long time since I have seen your dear face.

I imagine that we shall enjoy here (far from courts and women) a great gossip. So run hither as soon as you are free! I kiss you on both cheeks.

Tenderest remembrances to all, especially to Toto.

I am a victim of the HHHHHATRED OF THE PRIESTS, having been cursed by them in two churches — Sainte-Clotilde and Trinity!! They accuse me of being the inventor of obscene travesties, and of wishing to restore paganism!

TO GEORGE SAND.
1866.

DEAR MADAME: I cannot tell you how much pleased I am that you fulfilled what you called a duty. The kindness of your heart has touched me and your sympathy has made me proud. That is all.

Your letter, which I have just received, adds to your article and even surpasses it, and I do not know what to say to you unless I say frankly that I love you for it!

It was not I that sent you a little flower in an envelope last September. But it is a strange coincidence that I received at the same time, sent in the same fashion, a leaf plucked from a tree.

As to your cordial invitation, I reply neither yes nor no, like a true Norman. I shall surprise you, perhaps, some day this summer. I have a great desire to see you and to talk with you.

It would be very sweet to me to have your portrait to hang upon my study wall in the country, where I often pass long months entirely alone. Is my request indiscreet? If not, I send you a thousand thanks in advance. Take them in addition to my others, which I reiterate.

## TO GEORGE SAND.

PARIS, 1866.

MOST certainly I count upon your visit at my private domicile. As for the inconveniences dreaded by the fair sex, you will not perceive more of them than have others (be sure of that). My little stories of the heart and of the sense do not come out of a back shop. But as it is a long distance from my home to yours, in order to save you a useless journey, let me meet you as soon as you arrive in Paris, and we will dine together all by ourselves with our elbows on the table!

I have sent Bouilhet your kind message.

At the present moment I am deafened by the crowd in the street under my window following the prize ox! And they say that intellect flourishes among the people of the street!


## TO GEORGE SAND.

CROISSET, *Tuesday*, 1866.

You are alone and sad where you are, and I am the same here. Whence come the black moods that sometimes sweep over us? They creep up like the rising tide and we are suddenly overwhelmed and must flee. My method is to lie flat on my back and do nothing, and the wave passes after a time.

My romance has been going badly for a quarter of an hour. Then, too, I have just heard of two deaths, that of Cormenin, a friend for the past twenty-five years, and of Gavarni. Other things have troubled me, too, but all this will soon pass over.

You do not know what it is to sit a whole day with your head in your hands, squeezing your unhappy brain in trying to find a word. Your ideas flow freely, incessantly, like a river. But with me they run slowly, like a tiny rill. I must have great works of art to occupy me in order to obtain a cascade. Ah! I know what they are — the terrors of *style!*

In short, I pass my life gnawing my heart and my brain — that is the real truth about your friend.

You ask whether he thinks sometimes of his old troubadour of the clock. He does, indeed! And he regrets him. Our little nocturnal chats were very charming. There were moments when I had to restrain myself to keep from babbling to you like a big baby.

Your ears must have burned last night. I dined with my brother and his family. We spoke of scarcely anyone but you, and everyone sang your praises, dear and well-beloved master!

I re-read, *à propos* of your last letter (and by a natural train of ideas), Father Montaigne's chapter entitled "Some Verses of Virgil." That which he says about chastity is precisely my own belief.

It is the effort that is difficult, and not abstinence in itself. Otherwise, it would be a curse to the flesh. Heaven knows whither this would lead. So, at the risk of eternal reiteration, and of being like Prudhomme, I repeat that your young man was wrong. If he had been virtuous up to twenty years of age, his action would be an ignoble libertinage at fifty. Everyone gets his deserts some time! Great natures, that are also good, are above all things generous, and do not calculate expense. We must laugh and weep, work, play, and suffer, so that we may feel the divine vibration throughout our being. That, I believe, is the characteristic of true manhood.

## TO GEORGE SAND.

CROISSET, *Saturday night,* 1866.

AT LAST I have it, that beautiful, dear, and illustrious face! I shall put it in a large frame and hang it on my wall, being able to say, as M. de Talleyrand said to Louis Philippe: "It is the greatest honour my house ever has received." Not quite appropriate, for you and I are better than those two worthies!

Of the two portraits, the one I like the better is the drawing by Couture. As to Marchal's conception, he has seen in you only "the good woman"; but I, who am an old romanticist, find in it "the head of the author" who gave me in my youth so many beautiful dreams!

## TO GEORGE SAND.

CROISSET, 1866.

I, â MYSTERIOUS being, dear master? What an idea! I find myself a walking platitude, and am sometimes bored to death by the *bourgeois* I carry about under my skin! Sainte-Beuve, between you and me, does not know me at all, whatever he may say. I even swear to you (by the sweet smile of your grand-daughter!) that I know few men less "vicious" than myself. I have dreamed much, but have done little. That which is deceptive to superficial observers is the discord between my sentiments and my ideas. If you wish to have my confession, I will give it frankly.

My sense of the grotesque has always restrained me from yielding to any inclination towards licentiousness. I maintain that cynicism protects chastity. We must discuss this matter at length (that is, if you choose) the next time we meet.

This is the programme that I propose to you. During the next month my house will be in some disorder. But towards the end of October, or at the beginning of November (after the production of Bouilhet's play), I hope nothing will prevent you from returning here with me, not for a day, as you say, but for a week at least. You shall have your room "with a round table and everything needful for writing." Is that agreeable?

About the fairy play [*The Castle of Hearts*] I thank you for your kindly offer of assistance. I will tell you all about the thing (I am writing it in collaboration with Bouilhet). But I believe it is a mere trifle, and I am divided between the desire to gain a few piastres and shame at the idea of exhibiting such a piece of frivolity.

I find you a little severe towards Brittany, but not towards the Bretons themselves, who appear to me a crabbed set of animals.

*À propos* of Celtic archæology, I published, in *l'Artiste,* in 1858, a marvellous tale about the rocking stones, but I have not a copy of the number, and do not even remember in which month it appeared.

I have read, continuously, the ten volumes of *l'Historie de Ma Vie,* of which I knew about two thirds, in fragments. That which struck me most forcibly was the account of life in the convent.

On all these matters I have stored up a quantity of observations to submit to you when we meet.

## TO GEORGE SAND.

CROISSET, *Saturday night,* 1866.

THE sending of the two portraits made me believe that you were in Paris, dear master, and I wrote you a letter which now awaits you at the Rue des Feuillantines.

I have not found my article on the dolmens. But I have the whole manuscript about my trip through Brittany among my unedited works. We shall have it to let our tongues loose upon while you are here. Take courage!

I do not experience, as you do, that feeling as of the beginning of a new life, the bewilderment of a fresh existence newly opening. On the contrary, it seems to me that I have always existed, and I possess recollections that go back to the time of the Pharaohs! I can see myself at various epochs in history very clearly, following various occupations, and placed in divers circumstances. The present individual is the product of my past individualities. I have been a boatman on the Nile; a *leno* at Rome during the time of the Punic wars; then a Greek rhetorician at Suburra, where I was devoured by bugs. I died, during the crusades, from eating grapes on the coast of Syria. I have been a pirate and a monk; a clown and a coachman. Perhaps, also, an emperor in the Orient!

Many things would explain themselves if we could only know our true genealogy. For, the elements that go to make a man being limited, the same combinations must reproduce themselves.

We must regard this matter as we regard many others. Each of us takes hold of it by only one end, and never fully understands it. The psychological sciences remain where they have always lain, in folly and in darkness. All the more so since they possess no exact nomenclature, and we are compelled to employ the same expression to signify the most diverse ideas. When we mix up the categories, good-bye to the *morale!*

Do you not find that, since '89, we struggle with trifles? Instead of continuing along the broad road, which was as wide and beautiful as a triumphal way, .we run off into narrow paths, or struggle in the mire. It might be wiser to return temporarily to d'Holbach. Before admiring Prudhon, we should know Turgot!

. But "Chic," that modern religion, what would become of that?

"Chic" (or "Chique") opinions: to support Catholicism, without believing a word of it; to approve of slavery; to praise the House of Austria; to wear mourning for Queen Amélie; to admire *Orphée aux Enfers;* to occupy oneself with agriculture; to talk "sport;" to be cold; to be idiot enough to regret the treaties of 1815. All this is the very newest thing!

Ah! You believe because I pass my life in trying to make harmonious phrases and to avoid assonances, that I do not form my own little judgments on the affairs of this world. Alas! I do, and sometimes I boil with rage at not being able to express them.

But enough of gossip, or I shall bore you.

Bouilhet's play will appear early in November. And we shall see each other in about a month from that time.

I embrace you tenderly, dear master!

## TO GEORGE SAND.

*Monday night,* 1866.

You are sad, my poor friend and dear master; I thought of you at once on learning of the death of Duveyrier. Since you loved him, I pity you. This loss is one of many. These deaths we feel in the depths of our hearts. Each of us carries within himself his own burial ground.

I am all *unscrewed* since your departure; it seems to me now as if ten years have passed since last I saw you. My only topic of conversation with my mother is yourself; we all cherish the thought of you here.

Under what constellation were you born, to have united in your person qualities so diverse, so numerous, and so rare? I hardly know how to characterise the sentiment I feel for you, but I bear you a *particular* tenderness, such as I never have felt for anyone else. We understand each other well, do we not? And that is charming!

I regretted you especially last night at ten o'clock. There was a fire on my wood-merchant's premises. The sky was rosy, and the Seine was the colour of gooseberry sirup. I worked at the pumps for three hours, and came home as weak as the Turk of the giraffe.

A journal of Rouen, the *Nouvelliste,* has mentioned your visit at Rouen, and in such terms that on Saturday, after you had gone, I met several worthy *bourgeois* who were indignant at me because I had not exhibited you! The most absurd remark was made by an old sub-prefect:—"Ah! if we had only known that she was here . . . we should have . . . we should have" . . . pause of five minutes, while he searched for a word—"we should have . . . *smiled!*" That would have been a great compliment, eh?

To love you "more" is difficult, but I embrace you tenderly. Your letter of this morning, so melancholy, has touched the depths of my heart. We are separated just at the time when we wish to say so many things. Not all doors have yet been opened between you and me. You inspire me with a deep respect, and I dare not question you.

## TO EDMOND AND JULES DE GONCOURT.

*Friday, one o'clock,* 1867.

My DEAR OLD BOYS! On arriving at Paris, the day before yesterday, I learned of your nomination through Scholl's article. So my pleasure was mingled with annoyance.

Then, last evening, the princess told me you were in Paris. If you were in the habit of opening your door to the people that knock at it, I should have presented myself at midnight, to embrace you.

How shall we meet?—for I must return this evening. It is not you, Edmond, I wish to compliment so much as Jules, to whom the nomination must give more pleasure than it gives to you. The fifteenth of next August will be the date for your turn, I suppose.

Adieu, dear old fellows, I embrace you both most tenderly.

I wrote to you at Trouville, *poste restante*. Have you received my letter?

P. S.—A sudden thought seizes me. What do you intend to do this evening? Where shall you be at five minutes before midnight? Is it not possible that I might dine with you? Where shall we see each other?

You know that this is worn as soon as the news is printed in the *Moniteur*. So here is a little gift from your friend. Cut the ribbon and wear it. Cut it in half, because there is enough for two.

## TO GEORGE SAND.

*Wednesday night,* 1867.

I HAVE followed your advice, dear master, and I have taken exercise!

Am I not good, eh?

Sunday evening, at eleven o'clock, there was such beautiful moonlight on the river and across the snow, that I was seized with a wild desire to go out and bestir myself; so I walked for two hours and a half, showing the scenery to myself, and imagining I was travelling in Russia or in Norway! When the waves rose and cracked the ice along the edges of the river, it was, without joking, really superb. Then I thought of you, and longed for your companionship.

I do not like to eat alone. I find it necessary to associate the idea of some one to the things that give

me pleasure. But the right "some one" is extremely
rare. I ask myself why I love you. Is it because you
are a great "man" or simply a charming being? I
do not know. The one thing I am sure of is that I
feel for you a particular sentiment which I cannot
define.

*A propos* of this, do you believe (you, who are a
master in psychology) that one ever loves two persons in the same way, or that one ever experiences
two identical sensations? I do not believe it, as I
maintain that the individual changes every moment of
his existence.

You write me such pretty things regarding "dis-
interested affection." They are very true, but the
contrary also is true. We always imagine God in
our own image. At the foundation of all our loves
and all our admirations we find — ourselves, or something resembling ourselves. But what matters it?—
if we are admirable!

My own *ego* overwhelms me for a quarter of an
hour. How heavily that rascal weighs upon me at
times. He writes too slowly, and does not *pose* the
least in the world when he complains about his
work. What a task! And what devil possessed him
to induce him to seek such a subject? You ought to
give me a recipe for writing faster; yet you complain
of having to seek fortune! You!

I have had a little note from Sainte-Beuve, reassur-
ing me as to his health, but rather sad in tone. He
seems to be very sorry not to be able to haunt the
woods of Cyprus. He is right, after all, or at least,
it seems right to him, which amounts to the same
thing. Perhaps I shall resemble him when I reach his
age, but somehow, I believe not. As I had not the

same kind of youth, my old age will probably be different.

This reminds me that I have sometimes dreamed of writing a book on Saint Périne. Champfleury has treated this subject very badly. I see nothing whatever in it of a comical nature; I should bring out its painful and lamentable character. I believe that the heart never grows old; there are people in whom it even grows stronger with age. I was drier and harsher at twenty than I am to-day. I have become softened and feminised by wear and tear, while others have hardened and withered, and that almost makes me indignant. I feel that I am becoming a *cow!* A mere nothing stirs my emotions; everything troubles and agitates me and shakes me as a reed is shaken in the north wind.

One word of yours, which I have just recollected, made me wish to re-read *The Fair Maid of Perth*. She was something of a coquette, whatever they say of her. That good fellow had some imagination, decidedly.

Now, adieu. Think of me! I send you my tenderest thoughts.


## TO GEORGE SAND.

*Wednesday night,* 1867.

DEAR MASTER, dear friend of the good God, "let us talk a little of Dozenval," let us growl about Monsieur Thiers! Could there ever be a more triumphant imbecile, a more abject fellow, a meaner *bourgeois!*

No, no words could ever give an idea of the nausea that overcomes me when I contemplate that old pump-kin of a diplomat, fattening his stupidity under the muck of the *bourgeoisie*. Would it be possible to treat with more naïve and more inappropriate uncere-moniousness, matters of religion, the people, liberty, the past and the future, national history and natural history, everything? He seems to me as eternal as mediocrity itself! He prostrates me! But the finest thing of all is the spectacle of the brave National Guards, whom he threw out in 1848, now beginning to applaud him! What absolute lunacy! It proves that everything depends upon temperament. Prosti-tutes — represented in this case by France — are said to have always a weakness for old rascals!

I shall attempt, in the third part of my romance (when I shall have had the reaction following the June days), to insinuate a panegyric about him, *à propos* of his book: *De la Propriété,* and I hope that he will be pleased with me!

What care should one take sometimes, in express-ing an opinion on things of this world, not to risk being considered an imbecile later? It is a rude prob-lem. It seems to me that the best way is to de-scribe, with the simplest precision, those things that exasperate one. The dissection itself is a vengeance!

Ah, well! it is not at him alone that I am enraged, nor at the others — it is at our people in general.

However, if we had spent our time in instructing the higher classes on the subject of agriculture; if we had thought more of our stomachs than of our heads, probably we should resemble him!

I have just read the preface of Buchez to his *His-toire parlementaire.* Like other similar publications, it is full of stupidities, of which we feel the weight to this day.

It is not kind to say I do not think of my "old troubadour;" of what else should I think? Of my little book, perhaps,—but that is more difficult and not nearly so agreeable.

How long do you remain at Cannes? After Cannes, does not one usually return to Paris? I shall be there towards the end of January.

In order that my book may be finished in the spring of 1869, from this time on, I shall not allow myself even a week's holiday. This is the reason why I do not go to Nohant. I am still on the history of the amazons. In order to draw the bow with the best effect, they used to cut off one breast! Was that a good way, after all?

Adieu, dear master; write to me. I embrace thee tenderly!

## TO JULES MICHELET.

*Wednesday,* 1868.

No, MY dear master, I have not received your book, but I have already read it, and am re-reading it. What a mountain is yours! Where will you stop?

I am overwhelmed by this mass of ideas, and amazed at their profundity.

I believe I never have read anything that impressed me more deeply than that part about the baths of Acqui. You bring the Pyrenees and the Alps before our very eyes. But in your company one is always on the heights!

The weighty romance in which you express an interest (weighty for me, while waiting to see what it will be for others!), will not be finished in less than a whole year. I am full of it now, in the history of '48. My profound conviction is that the clergy has acted amazingly.

The dangers of democratic Catholicism, pointed out by you in the preface to your *Revolution*, are already here. Ah! we are indeed alone. But you remain to us, you!

I clasp your hand warmly, and beg you to believe me yours, with true affection.

## TO GEORGE SAND.

CROISSET, *Wednesday evening, Sept.* 9, 1868.

Is THIS handsome conduct, dear master? Two months have passed since you wrote last to your old troubadour! Are you in Paris, Nohant, or where?

They say that *Cadio* is being rehearsed at the Porte Saint-Martin (are you very sorry, you and Chilly?). They say also, that Thuillier will make her reappearance in your play. (I thought she was dying —I mean Thuillier, not your play.) And when will *Cadio* be produced. Are you pleased?

I live absolutely like an oyster. My romance is the rock to which I cling, and I know nothing of what is going on in the world. I do not even read, or rather, I read only the *Lanterne.* Rochefort bores me, to tell the truth. One must, however, have considerable bravery to dare to say, even timidly, that perhaps he is not the first writer of the century! O *Velches! Velches!* as Monsieur de Voltaire would sigh, or rather, roar!

And Sainte-Beuve — do you see him? I am working furiously. I have just written a description of the forest of Fontainebleau, which has filled me with a desire to hang myself on one of its trees! I was interrupted for three weeks, and had a hard task to put myself in train to work again. I have the peculiarity of a camel — I find it difficult to stop when once I get started, and hard to start after I have been resting. I have worked steadily for a year at a time. After which I loafed definitely, like a *bourgeois*. It was difficult at first, and not at all pleasant. It is time now that I should do something fine, something that shall please me. That which would please me greatly for a quarter of an hour would be to embrace you! When shall I be able to do so? From now until that time, I send you a thousand sweet thoughts.

TO MAXIME DUCAMP.

CROISSET, *July 23,* 1869.

MY GOOD OLD MAX: I feel the need of writing you a long letter. I do not know whether I shall have strength, but I will try.

Since his return to Rouen, after receiving his nomination for the place of librarian (August, 1867), our poor Bouilhet was convinced that he should leave his bones there. Everyone, including myself, pitied him for his sadness. He did not appear the man he was formerly; he was completely changed, except for his literary intelligence, which remained the same. In short, when I returned to Paris, in June, I found him a lamentable figure. A journey that he made to Paris on account of his *Mademoiselle Aïssé,* because the manager demanded that certain changes be made in the second act, was so difficult for him that he could scarcely drag himself to the theatre.

On visiting him at his house, the last Sunday in June, I found Dr. P—— of Paris, X—— of Rouen, Morel, the alienist, and a good chemist, one of Bouilhet's friends, named Dupré. Bouilhet dared not ask for a consultation with my brother, realising that he was very ill and fearing to hear the truth.

Dr. P—— sent him to Vichy, whence Villemain hastened to despatch him back to Rouen. On debarking at Rouen, he finally summoned my brother. The evil was found to be irreparable, as indeed Villemain had written me.

During these last two weeks my mother has been at Verneuil, at the house of the Mesdames V——, and letters have been delayed three days, so you see what anxiety I have had. I went to see Bouilhet both days that he was here, and observed some amelioration in his condition. His appetite was excellent, as well as his courage, and the tumour on his leg had diminished.

His sisters came from Carny in order to speak to him of religious matters, and were so violent that they really scandalised a worthy canon of the cathedral. Our poor Bouilhet was superb—he sent them packing! When I left him for the last time, on Saturday, he had a volume of Lamettrie on his night-table, which recalled to my mind my poor friend Alfred Le Poittevin reading Spinoza. No priest was summoned. His anger against his sisters appeared to sustain him until Saturday, and then I departed for Paris, in the hope that he would live a long time.

On Sunday, at five o'clock, he became delirious, and recited aloud the scenario of a drama of the Middle Ages on the Inquisition. He called for me, in order to show it to me, and was very enthusiastic over it. Then a trembling seized him; he murmured, "Adieu! Adieu!" His head sank under Léonie's chin, and he died very quietly. Monday morning my porter awakened me with a telegram that announced the death in the usual terse fashion of a despatch. I was alone; I packed my things, sent the news to you, and went to tell it to Duplan, who was engaged in his business affairs. Then I walked the streets an hour, and it was very hot near the railway station. From Paris to Rouen in a coach filled with people. Opposite me was a damsel that smoked cigarettes, stretched her feet out on the seat and sang.

When I saw once more the towers of Mantes I thought I should go mad, and I believe I was not far from it. Seeing me very pale, the damsel offered me her *eau de Cologne*. It revived me a little, but what a thirst! That of the desert of Sahara was nothing to it. At last I arrived at the Rue de Bihorel; but here I will spare you details.

I never met a better fellow than little Philip; he and that good Léonie took admirable care of Bouilhet. I approved of everything they had done. In order to reassure Bouilhet, and to persuade him that he was not dangerously ill, Léonie had refused to marry him, and her son encouraged her in this resistance. This marriage was so much the fixed intention of Bouilhet, however, that he had had all the necessary papers drawn. As for the young man, I found that he had behaved in every way like a gentleman.

D'Osmoy and I conducted the ceremonies. A great many persons came to the funeral, two thousand at least; the prefect, the procurer-general, etc.,— all the little dignitaries! Would you believe that even while following his coffin, I realised keenly the grotesqueness of the ceremony? I fancied I could hear him speaking to me; I felt that he was there, at my side, and it seemed as if he and I were following the corpse of some one else! The weather was very hot, threatening a storm. I was covered with perspiration, and the walk to the cemetery finished me. His friend Caudron had chosen the spot for the grave, near that of Flaubert senior. I leaned against a railing to breathe. The coffin stood on the trestles over the grave. The discourses began (there were three!); then I fainted, and my brother and a stranger took me away.

The next day I went to my mother, at Serquigny. Yesterday I went to Rouen, to take charge of Bouilhet's papers; to-day I have read the letters that have been sent to me, and oh! dear Max, it was hard!

In his will he left instructions to Léonie that all his books and papers should be given to Philip, charging the latter to consult with four friends in order to decide what to do with the unedited works: myself, D'Osmoy, you, and Caudron. He left a volume of excellent poems, four plays in prose, and *Mademoiselle*

*Aïssé.* The manager of the Odéon does not like the second act of this play; I do not know what he will do.

It will be necessary for you and D'Osmoy to come here this winter, so that we may decide what shall be published. My head troubles me too much for me to continue now, and besides, what more can I say?

Adieu! I embrace you tenderly. There is only you now, only you! Do you remember when we wrote *Solus ad solum?*

In all the letters I have received I find this phrase: "We must close up our ranks." One gentleman, whom I do not know, has sent his card, with these two words: *Sunt lacrymæ!*

## TO EDMOND DE GONCOURT.

*Sunday evening,* 1870.

How I pity you, my poor friend! Your letter overcame me this morning. Except for the personal confidence you made me (which you may be sure I shall keep), it told me nothing new, or rather, I mean that I had guessed all that you wrote me. I think of you every day and many times a day. The memory of my lost friends leads me fatally to the thought of you! The schedule has been well filled during the past year— your brother, Bouilhet, Sainte-Beuve, and Duplan! My dreams are darkened by the shadows of tombs, among which I walk.

But I dare not complain to you; for your grief must surpass all those one could feel or imagine.

Do you wish me to speak of myself, my dear Edmond? Well, I am engrossed in a work that gives me much pain,—it is the preface to Bouilhet's book. I have glided over the biographical part as much as possible. I shall write more at length after an examination of his works, and still more upon his (or our) literary doctrines.

I have re-read all that he ever wrote. I have run through our old letters. I have found a series of souvenirs, some of which are thirty years old. It is not very cheerful work, as you may imagine! And besides, here at Croisset, I am pursued by his phantom, which I find behind every bush in the garden, on the divan in my study, and even among my garments — in my dressing-gown, which sometimes he used to wear.

I hope to think less about him when this sad work is finished,—in about six weeks. After that I shall try to re-write *Saint Antony*, although my heart is not in it now. You know well that one always writes with the thought of some particular person in view.

The particular person being, for me, no more, my courage fails me.

I live alone here with only my mother, who grows visibly older from day to day. It has become impossible to hold any serious conversation with her, and I have no one to whom I can talk.

I hope to go to Paris in August, and then I shall see you. But where shall you be? Write to me about yourself sometimes, my poor Edmond! No one pities you more than I. I embrace you warmly.

## TO GEORGE SAND.

*Sunday, June 26,* 1870.

SOMEONE forgets her old troubadour, who has just come from the funeral of a friend. Of the seven friends that used to gather at the Magny dinners, only three remain! I am stuffed with coffins, like an old churchyard! I have had enough of it, frankly!

Yet in the midst of all this, I go on working! I finished last night the preface to my poor Bouilhet's book. I intend to see whether some means may not be found to produce a comedy of his in prose. After that I shall take up *Saint Antony* once more.

And you, dear master, what has become of you and yours? My niece is in the Pyrenees, and I live here alone with my mother, who grows more and more deaf, so that my existence is far from lively. I should go to some warmer climate. But to do that I have neither time nor money. So I must erase and re-write, and dig away as hard as possible.

I shall go to Paris early in August. I shall stay here through October, in order to see the performance of *Aïssé*. My absence will be limited to a week at Dieppe about the end of the month. These are my projects.

The funeral of Jules de Goncourt was very sad. Théo was there and shed floods of tears.

## TO MADAME REGNIER.

*Thursday evening, 7 o'clock,* 1871.

DEAR MADAME:    I have had to occupy me during the last few weeks

*First:* the arrangements regarding Bouilhet's tomb;

*Second:* plans about his monument;

*Third:* looking after his volume of poems, which has just gone to press;

*Fourth:* finding an engraver to make his portrait;

*Fifth:* all my time for two weeks was taken up with *Aïssé,* I shall read it to-morrow to the actors. The rehearsals will begin next Saturday, and the play will be produced about the first of January.

I was obliged to leave Croisset so unexpectedly that my servant and my belongings will not arrive until three days later.    A detailed account of the intrigues I have had to demolish would fill a volume.

I have engaged the actors.    I have worked myself on the costumes at the Cabinet des Estampes; in short, I have not had a moment's rest for two weeks ; and this petty life, so exasperating and so busy, will last at this rate at least two full months.

What a world!    I am not surprised that it killed my good Bouilhet!    Besides, I have re-written my preface to his books, as it displeased me in its former state.

I beg you, for heaven's sake, to give me a little liberty for the moment, because with the best will in the world, it is impossible for me to do everything at once.    I must attend first to the most pressing affairs. Besides, you are wrong to wish to publish *now.*

What good will it do? Where would you find readers?

I do not hide from you the fact that I find rather unjust your amiable reproaches regarding the voyage to Mantes. Why can you not understand that it would be very painful to me to go to Mantes? Every time I pass before the buffet, I turn away my head! Nevertheless, I will keep my promise. But it would be easier for me to go from Paris to Mantes than to stop there in passing. Do not be vexed with me any longer; pity me, rather!

## TO GEORGE SAND.

*Tuesday, April* 16, 1872.

DEAR GOOD MASTER: I ought to have replied at once to your first letter, so sweet and tender. But I was too sad. The physical force to do it failed me.

To-day, at last, I have begun to hear the birds sing and to notice the green leaves. The sunshine no longer irritates me, which is a good sign. If I could only follow my inclination to travel, I should be saved.

Your second letter (that of yesterday) moved me to tears. How good you are! What a kind heart! I have no need of money just at present, thank you. But if I were in need of it, I should certainly ask you for it.

My mother left Croisset to Caroline, on condition that I should retain my apartments there. So until the complete liquidation of the succession, I shall remain here. Before deciding upon the future, I must know what I shall have to live upon; after that, we shall see.

Shall I have the courage to live absolutely alone in a solitary place? I doubt it. I am growing old. Caroline cannot live here now. She has two places already, and the house at Croisset is expensive to keep up.

I believe that I shall give up my lodgings in Paris. Nothing calls me there any more. All my friends are dead, and the last, my poor Théo, is not likely to be here long. I fear it! Ah, it is hard to make oneself over at fifty years!

I have realised during the last two weeks that my poor good mamma was the being I have loved most! To lose her is like tearing away a part of my own body.

## TO THE BARONESS LEPIC.

AT MY HERMITAGE,

September 14 (the month called Boédromion by the Greeks), 1872.

I TAKE up my pen to write to you, and, shutting myself up in the silence of my study, I permit myself, O beautiful lady, to burn at your feet some grains of purest incense!

I say to myself: She has gone to the new Athens with the foster-sons of Mars! Their limbs are covered with brilliant blue, while I wear a rustic coat! Glittering swords dangle at their sides, while I carry only my pens! Plumes ornament their heads, while I have scarcely any hair! Many cares and much study have ravished from me that crown of youth — that forest which the hand of Time, the destroyer, strips from our brows.

This is the reason why my breast is torn by blackest jealousy, O lovely lady!

But your missive, thank the gods! came to me like a refreshing breeze, like a veritable perfume of dittany.

If I could only have the certainty of seeing you, at no distant time, amid our fields, settled near us! The rigour of the approaching blasts of winter would be softened by your presence.

As to the political outlook, your anxieties are, perhaps, greater than they need be. We must hope that our great national historian will close, for a time, the era of revolutions. May we see the doors of the temple of Janus shut forever! That is the desire of my heart, as a friend of the arts and of innocent gaiety.

Ah, if all men, fleeing the pomp of courts and the agitations of the Forum, would listen to the simple voice of nature, there would be only happiness here below, the dances of shepherds, fond embraces beneath the trees on one side and another — here, there, everywhere! But my ideas run away with me.

Will Madame your mother devote herself always to the occupations of Thalia? Very well! She proposes to face the public in the house of Molière. I comprehend that, but I believe it would be better (in the interest of her dramatic lucubration) if I myself should take this fruit of her muse to the director of that establishment. Then, as soon as I should arrive in the capital, I should make my toilet, call my servant and command him to go and find a coach for me ìn the public square; I should enter the vehicle, drive through the streets, arrive at the Théâtre Française, and finish by finding our man. All this would be for me only the affair of a moment!

In declaring myself, Madame, your unworthy slave, I depose                              PRUD' HOMME.

TO EMILE ZOLA.

CROISSET, near Rouen, *June 3*, 1874.

I HAVE read it — *La Conquête de Plassans* — read it all at one breath, as one swallows a glass of good wine; then I ruminated over it, and now, my dear friend, I can talk sensibly about it. I feared, after the *Ventre de Paris,* that you would bury yourself in the "system" in your resolution. But no! You are a good fellow! And your latest book is a fine, swaggering production!

Perhaps it fails in making prominent any special place, or having a central scene (a thing that never happens in real life), and perhaps also there is a little too much dialogue among the accessory characters. There! in picking you to pieces carefully, these are the only defects I discover. But what power of observation! what depth! what a masterly hand!

That which struck me most forcibly in the general tone of the work was the ferocity of passion underlying the surface of good-fellowship. That is very strong, old friend, very strong and broad, and well sustained.

What a perfect *bourgeois* is Mouret, with his curiosity, his avarice, his resignation, and his flatness!

The Abbé Faujas is sinister and great — a true director! How well he manages the woman, how ably he makes himself her master, first in taking her up through charity, and then in brutalising her!

As to her (Marthe), I cannot express to you how much I admire her, and the art displayed in developing her character, or rather her malady. Her hysteric state and her final avowal are marvellous. How well you describe the breaking-up of the household!

I forgot to mention the Tronches, who are adorable ruffians, and the Abbé Bouvelle, who is exquisite with his fears and his sensibility.

Provincial life, the little gardens, the Paloque family, the Rastoil, and the tennis-parties, — perfect, perfect!

Your treatment of details is excellent, and you use the happiest words and phrases: "The tonsure like a cicatrice;" "I should like it better if he went to see the women;" "Mouret had stuffed the stove," etc.

And the circle of youth — that was a true invention! I have noted many other things on the margins, viz.:

The physical details which Olympe gives regarding her brother; the strawberry; the mother of the abbé ready to become his pander; and her old trunk.

The harshness of the priest, who waves away the handkerchief of his poor sweetheart, because he detects thereon "an odour of woman."

The description of the sacristy, with the name of M. Delangre on the wall — the whole phrase is a jewel.

But that which surpasses everything, that which crowns the whole work, is the end! I know of nothing more powerful than that *dénouement*. Marthe's visit at her uncle's house, the return of Mouret, and his inspection of the house! One is seized by fear, as in the reading of some fantastic tale, and one arrives at this effect by the tremendous realism, the intensity of truth. The reader feels his head turned, in sympathy with Mouret.

The insensibility of the *bourgeois,* who watches the fire seated in his armchair, is charming, and you wind up with one sublime stroke: the apparition of the *soutane* of the Abbé Serge at the bedside of his dying mother, as a consolation or a chastisement!

There is one bit of chicanery, however. The reader (that has no memory) does not know by instinct what motive prompts M. Rougon and Uncle Macquart to act as they do. Two paragraphs of explanation would have been sufficient.

Never mind! it is what it is, and I thank you for the pleasure it has given me.

Sleep on both ears, now your work is done!

Lay aside for me all the stupid criticisms it draws forth. That kind of document interests me very much.

## TO GUY DE MAUPASSANT.

DIEPPE, *July* 28, 1874.

MY DEAR FRIEND: As Saturday is for you a kind of consecrated day, and as I could be in Paris only one day, which was last Saturday, I shall not be able to see you on your return from Helvetia.

Know, then, that *Le Sexe Faible* was enthusiastically received at the Cluny Theatre, and it will be acted there after Zola's piece, that is, about the last of November.

Winschenk, the director of this little box of a theatre, predicts a great pecuniary success. Amen!

It goes without saying, it is the general opinion that I lower myself in making my appearance in an inferior theatre. But this is the story: Among the artists engaged by Winschenk for my play was Mlle. Alice Regnault. He feared that she would be taken by the Vaudeville Theatre, and that the Vaudeville would not allow her to appear in my play. Will you be kind enough to inform yourself discreetly of the state of the case when you are in Paris?

I shall return to Croisset Friday evening, and Saturday I shall begin *Bouvard et Pécuchet*. I tremble at the prospect, as one would the night before embarking for a voyage around the world!

All the more reason why we should meet and embrace.


TO MAURICE SAND.

CROISSET, *Sunday, June* 24, 1876.

YOU have forestalled me, my dear Maurice! I wished to write to you, but I waited until you should be a little more free, more alone. I thank you for your kind thought.

Yes, there are few of us left now. And if I do not remain here long, it is because my former friends have drawn me to them.

This has seemed to me like burying my mother a second time. Poor, dear, great woman! What genius and what a heart! But she lacked nothing; it is not she who calls for pity!

What shall you do now? Shall you remain at Nohant? That dear old house must seem terribly empty to you. But you, at least, are not alone. You have a wife—a rare woman!—and two exquisite children. While I was with you there, I felt above all my sadness, two desires: to run away with Aurore, and to kill Monsieur . . . ! That is the truth: it is useless to try to analyse the psychology of the thing.

I received yesterday a very tender letter from the good Tourgueneff. He, too, loved her! But who did not love her? If you had beheld the grief of Martine in Paris! It was overwhelming.

Plauchut is still at Nohant, I suppose. Tell him I love him after seeing him weep so bitterly.

And let your own tears flow freely, my dear friend! Do not try to console yourself—it would be almost impossible. Some day you will find within yourself a deep and sweet certainty that you were always a good son, and that she knew it well. She spoke of you as a blessing.

And after you shall have joined her once more, and after the great-grandchildren of the grandchildren of your two little daughters also shall have rejoined her, and when for a long time people have ceased to talk of the things and the persons that surround us at present — in some centuries to come — there will still be hearts that will palpitate at her words! People will read her books, will ponder over her thoughts, will love as she loved.

But all that *does not give her back to you!* With what shall we sustain ourselves, then, if pride fails us,

and what man can feel more of that for his mother
than yourself?

Now, my dear friend, adieu! When shall we
meet again? For I feel an insatiable desire to talk
of *her!*

Embrace Madame Maurice for me, as I embraced
her on the stairs at Nohant, also your little ones.

Yours, from the depths of my heart.

\

## TO GUY DE MAUPASSANT.

*Night of August 28,* 1876.

YOUR letter has rejoiced me, young man! But I
advise you to moderate yourself, in the interest of
literature.

Take care! all depends upon the end one wishes
to attain. A man who has accredited himself an artist
has no right to live like other men.

All that which you tell me about Catulle Mendès
does not surprise me at all. He wrote to me the
day before yesterday, to ask me to give him *gratis*
the fragments of the *Château des Cœurs,* and also
the unedited stories that I had just finished. I replied that it was quite impossible, which is true.
Yesterday I wrote him a rather sharp letter, as I was
indignant at the article on Renan. It attacked him
in the grossest fashion, and there was also some
humbug about Berthelot. Have you read it, and what
do you think of it? In short, I said to Catulle, first,
that I wished him to efface my name from the list
of his collaborators; and, second, not to send me his

journal any more! I do not wish to have anything in common with such fellows! It is a very bad set, my dear friend, and I advise you to do as I have done—let them entirely alone. Catulle will probably reply to my letter, but my decision is taken, and that is an end of it. That which I cannot pardon is the base democratic envy.

The tiresome article on Offenbach goes to the extremest limits about his comic spirit. And what stupidity! I mean the joke that was invented by Fiorantino in 1850, and is still alive to-day!

In order to make a triad, add the name of Littré, the gentleman who pretends that we are all descended from apes; and last Friday the butchery of Sainte-Beuve! Oh, the idiocy of it!

As to myself, I am working very hard, seeing no one, reading no journals, and bawling away like a maniac in the seclusion of my study. I pass the whole day, and almost the whole night, bent over my table, and admire the sunrise with great regularity! Before my dinner (about seven o'clock) I splash about in the *bourgeoise* waves of the Seine.—*À propos* of health, you do not appear to me to look very ill. All the better! Think no more about it!

## TO GUY DE MAUPASSANT.

*Wednesday night,* 1880.

MY DEAR FRIEND: I do not know yet what day De Goncourt, Zola, Alphonse Daudet and Charpentier will come here to breakfast and dine, and perhaps to sleep. They must decide this evening, so that I may know by Friday morning. I think they will come on Monday. If your eye will permit you then, kindly transport your person to the dwelling of one of these rascals, learn when they expect to leave, and come along with them.

Should they all pass Monday night at Croisset, as I have only four beds to offer, you will take that of the *femme de chambre*—who is absent just now.

Commentary: I have conjured up so many alarms and improbabilities regarding your malady, that I should be glad, purely for my own satisfaction, to have you examined by *my* Doctor Fortin, a simple health officer, but a man I consider very able.

Another observation: If you have not the where-withal to make the journey, I have a superb double louis at your service. To refuse through mere delicacy would be a very stupid thing to do!

A last note: Jules Lemaître, to whom I have promised your protection in regard to Graziani, will present himself at your place. He has talent and is a true littérateur,—a *rara avis,* to whom we must give a cage larger than Havre.

Perhaps he too will come to Croisset on Monday; and as it is my intention to stuff you all, I have invited Doctor Fortin, so then he may extend his services to the sick ones!

The festival would lack much in splendour if my "disciple" were not there.          Thy old friend.

P. S.—I received this morning an incomprehensible letter, four pages long, signed Harry Alis. It appears that I have wounded him! How? In any case, I shall ask his pardon. *Vive* the young bloods!

I have re-read *Boule de Suif*, and I maintain that it is a masterpiece. Try to write a dozen stories like that, and you will be a man! The article by Wolff has filled me with joy! O eunuchs!

Madame Brainne has written me that she was enchanted with it. So did Madame Lapierre!

You will remember that you promised me to make some inquiries of D'Aurevilly. He has written this of me: "Can no one persuade M. Flaubert not to write any more?" It might be a good time now to make certain extracts from this gentleman's works. There is need of it!

How about the *Botanique?* How is your health? And how goes the volume of verse?

Sarah Bernhardt seems to me gigantic! And the "fathers of families" petition for the congregations!

Decidedly, this is a farcical epoch!

www.ingramcontent.com/pod-product-compliance
Lightning Source LLC
Chambersburg PA
CBHW030344030726
47499CB00003B/893